It's All About The Shoes

by Laura Laffoon

Susan ~
Be EXtraordinary!
Laura

Susan —

extraordinary!

[signature]

Table of Contents

Preface

Several years ago I lost a dear friend to cancer. Karen Haas Smith was an amazing woman who served an extraordinary God whom she clung to until her last breath. Her journey ended far too early, yet the people touched along the way will never forget the impact she had on their lives. I am one of those touched by her life.

On my first day of college, I was a nervous somewhat frightened 17 year old venturing from home for the first time. I was greeted by Karen and her huge bright smile as we met in the lobby of our dorm, MacGregor Hall. We talked about where we were from, why we chose Montreat Anderson College and what we were excited to experience in college. From the moment I saw Karen, I knew we would be friends.

Shortly after classes started, cheerleading tryouts were held and Karen and I both tried out. We made the team and were looking forward to cheering together. I had never cheered before in fact tried out in high school but never made the team. They said I was not loud enough-apparently they didn't know me very well! Karen and I cheered together for 2 years at MAC. Then we both transferred to the same college in Jackson, Mississippi, Belhaven University. Karen continued to cheer but I pursued another path-soccer.

Even though our hobbies and friend groups took us down different paths we could always search each other out to vent and dream about the men in our lives, our classes, and our futures.

We went our separate ways at Belhaven but always remained friends.

Karen was a great encourager for me as I discovered who I was as a person and as a follower of Jesus. Her love for Jesus and for people around her was contagious! Karen's life was truly extraordinary.

In writing this book, I want to encourage you to be all God created you to be. To see yourself through the eyes of the God who uniquely created you to do something utterly amazing for His kingdom. Karen was a woman who embraced all her God-given gifts, she served Him with those gifts, embodied as a loving wife, wonderful mother, and loyal friend.

You can live an extraordinary life, living out God's purpose for you! We are all on a journey. All of our journeys are different. We have different gifts and abilities. We have lived different stories. We all have different purposes.

We all walk this journey called life. I have chosen to write this book using shoes as a metaphor. I happen to love shoes! When I look at my shoes, I see different parts of my life, my journey, my story.

As you read this book, I hope you are inspired to leave the ordinary life behind and become the extraordinary woman God created you to be!

Shoe Closet

One Saturday afternoon snuggled under my plush cheetah print blanket with coffee in hand, I found myself flipping through countless catalogs. I love collecting all the catalogs that come in a week and taking time on Saturday to look thru them all very diligently to make sure I am not missing anything I might need! Pouring over the catalog is cheaper than going to the actual store. I mark the items I love and must have, but never really purchase!

On this particular perusing excursion I was looking through a Macy's catalog filled with all kinds of trinkets and gift items. Slowly turning each page, being careful not to miss any lovely gift for someone I *might* know, I stopped and there it was! My life changed forever at that moment!

I did not see the color of the plate, the cost of the plate, nor did I check whether a 50% discount was available to acquire the plate. All I saw were the words imprinted on the plate!

" Masquerading as the ordinary is exhausting"

Finally a store had captured my heart's motto! My husband, Jay, would tell you that many stores capture my heart! But this was different. I knew in my soul that this is how I would forever live my life. Now before you call me melodramatic or a little over the top (because if you knew me you would know that neither of those words are commonly associated with me), you should know that one of my highest values in life is uniqueness. These words captured that value precisely!

Since that Saturday, I have lived life striving to be extraordinary and no longer masquerading as ordinary is not always easy. Ordinary is easy and accepted. A desire to want to be extraordinary, can, at times, be seen by others as an oddity, nonconforming, atypical and or incredulous! It means walking away from life as others see it and striving for something more. I don't want to be like everyone else! I want to be the woman, wife, mom, and friend, God created me to be.

I was created by an extraordinary God, to be an extraordinary woman, and live an extraordinary life, for Him.

My goal in writing this book is to help you walk away from an ordinary life and live the extraordinary life you were created to live! God has created us each with our own set of gifts and abilities – much like we each have our own taste in shoes and what we desire to put on our feet. For example, I am a barefoot sandal lovin' girl. My feet feel claustrophobic in shoes that don't allow my toes to peek out! I have a girlfriend who doesn't enjoy wearing sandals because her feet get dirty. She prefers the protection of close-toed shoes!

> *I was created by an extraordinary God, to be an extraordinary woman, and live an extraordinary life, for Him.*

Moving from ordinary to extraordinary involves discovering who we were created to be and what we were created to do for God's kingdom. Shoes are one way we express our uniqueness and the woman we are inside. It may be painful at times and You may be seen by others as odd. But strap on your shoes, tie up your laces, and let's get moving from ordinary to extraordinary!

Let's Explore Our Shoe Closet

Let's take a look at what shoes you will need to begin your extraordinary journey. Close your eyes and imagine your shoe closet. Now, some of you are saying right now, " Laura, I don't have a shoe *closet*". Well neither do I but I do have shoes in my closet!

Wouldn't it be magical to have an entire closet filled with shoes, organized by use and color, with shelves that are stacked to the ceiling, that can pivot allowing you to select the perfect pair?

When you close your eyes and visualize your shoes…what do you see? In my closet, there is an entire basket of sandals contrasted by a shelf of high heels that I wear on stage, along with essential loafers and tennis shoes. Gandering at my shoes, you would see relaxing shoes are my favorite! You would also see a desire to be unique in the heels I wear on stage! I consider it my duty to shop and shop until I find *THE* pair that no one else will
4

have!

As women we unnecessarily spend countless hours trying to be something or someone we are not. Let's be honest! We pay to have our hair color of choice. We run, walk, lift weights, practice yoga, and heft a kettle ball to keep up with the latest trending movie star. We spread hot wax all over our face and then rip it off, in order to have the smooth skin we had when we were born! Some magazine articles describe women who have had their foot bone shaved in order to accommodate their stylish shoes! Yet we do not spend time reflecting on the gifts and abilities that our extraordinary God packaged within us. Competition to be seen as fabulous starts early in our lives.

When I was in high school, my youth pastor, Chris Halverson, challenged me by asking me what I wanted to do with my life. My response was that I would love to go to New York and be a model. His unforgettable words touched my soul. " Laura, you have been made for something so much more than that". The realization Chris brought to light was that I had been given unique gifts and abilities by a God who needed me to do something much different than modeling. I was not genetically designed to be tall and thin! I simply loved shopping and clothes!

As a result I took that summer and did an internship with the youth department at my church and discovered that God had equipped me with a heart for ministry. My gifts and abilities were much more aligned with ministry than modeling.

As a teenager, every Saturday was spent with my "besties" hanging out at the local mall. We would window shop, try on clothes, consume junk food, and rate cute boys. One memorable trip involved dancing in the water fountains but that is another story!

At that time my family budget could not afford many extras in life. I remember vividly those Saturdays flipping thru clothes racks wishing I had an endless supply of money to purchase the latest fashion ensemble. I vividly remember telling myself that if I could afford those items I would be the most popular girl at school, have tons of friends, date the cutest boy and might even be homecoming queen! BUT I needed to have the best clothes because with out the clothes I was nothing. What a lie we believe! Moving from the ordinary to the extraordinary is realizing that clothes don't make the woman -neither do shoes. The difference is a heart that runs to God, fervently chasing after Him and the life He wants for you!

After the conversation with Chris, I began to look deeper. What were my abilities? What were my gifts? How had God uniquely equipped me?

Every one of us has been uniquely and individually created! We can understand and embrace our uniqueness by answering these 3 questions leaving the ordinary behind and move onto our extraordinary life.

- Who am I?
- Where am I?
- What am I becoming?

> *Every one of us has been uniquely and individually created!*

The answers, believe it or not, are found in your shoe closet.

Who Am I?

This is certainly not a new question to any of us! We have all pondered this at some point in our lives, probably more than once. By middle school we are trying to figure out in what group we want to be included. Are we an athlete or math-athlete? In high school, those friend groups change, again we ask, " Who am I"? Moving into the college years, the question re-surfaces based on our study track or vocational choices. Unfortunately, it doesn't stop there! At 53, I still ask that question! Each phase of life brings new opportunities, yet the same question.

In 6th grade, Grace was in what she would term the "nerd group". Her friends were very academically competitive in school and within the group. Sports was not in her vocabulary . In fact we joke in our house that if it involves a ball she is not playing! She began swimming in 4th grade, but would not call herself an athlete by any stretch of the imagination!

As she entered 7th grade, as a family we chose homeschooling. Our touring calendar took us to San Diego, Arizona,

Nevada, Florida, and many places in between and we didn't want her to miss out!

We had a great year traveling and experiencing many things few people have the opportunity to explore. Grace began swimming competitively that year and as she participated in a few swim meets she found her niche. The following year not only had the travel experiences the past year given her a broader world view than her peers, but her "nerd" friends had moved on. Her self worth was found in hanging out with swimmers and athletes in general. She practiced with the high school swim team and a year later joined the team.

As a result of life's circumstances, Grace found out that who she was had changed dramatically. Answering the question again in 8th grade, the answer would be, "I am a swimmer". (But still not an athlete, in her mind!)

"Who am I", is a question of identity. It is the beginning of your story, your journey to move from ordinary to extraordinary. Take a moment to ask the question for yourself. Who am I?

My Dad

Born in Grantville, GA. Charles Gregory Bass, Sr. was the son of Charles T and Rhodelle Flourney Bass.

I never knew my paternal grandparents as my grandmother died when my dad was still very young and my grandfather while he was a young boy. My Dad was raised by his oldest sister, Elizabeth. As the youngest of 6 living in rural southern Georgia, in the 1930's, he was an orphan.

Franklin Delano Roosevelt was President at the time, and my daddy shared his struggle as he contracted polio at 6. FDR built The Little White House in Warm Springs, Georgia, when he was governor of New York as a retreat from the paralysis of Polio. Nearby, a rehabilitation facility was built and that is where my daddy was introduced to FDR. A story he loved to tell!

Daddy always walked with a cane because the polio had left him with a good leg and a bad "shorter" leg. In his early 20's he was diagnosed with Juvenile diabetes and in my lifetime alone, he had 4 heart attacks and 3 strokes. While terrifying, the

7

scariest times I remember as a child were when my daddy would have a "reaction" as a result of his diabetes. We would literally have to pour Orange Juice down his throat or force feed him a Hershey's candy bar to raise his blood sugar.

In my late teens, dad slipped and broke his good leg. Never again did he walk without crutches. Retiring at an early age due to complications from pneumonia, in his last years he became chemically imbalanced due to the side effects of multiple medications.

The last time I ever saw him, my sister and I were heading to Florida to visit my Mammaw. Leaving the house, we didn't kiss him, but just said goodbye because he had covered his head with a blanket "watching" television. The chemical imbalance, made him at times, what we lovingly referred to as "crazy in the head"-thus the blanket over the head!

Unlike other daddies he couldn't run or ride bikes with us. He would play catch or football in the yard but did not run or tackle us. Some of my fondest memories are of him sitting in his chair outside watching us play. When my younger brother and I would argue he would stick us outside and say " Duke it out". We never did.

Though different than other daddies, he was extraordinary. His nickname was Sonny because a smile always graced his face. He sang in our church's choir, and I loved to see him the choir loft, belting out the notes! He had a beautiful voice, and when he sang his entire face lit up. He was hard headed and stubborn, but his smile would light up a room. He may not have been like other dads but he was *my* daddy.

The summer before my senior year in college, my daddy passed away. I wasn't mad at God when he passed, I just had many questions. Having been the first child in my family to graduate from college, I very much wanted to make my daddy proud as he watched me receive my diploma. Why God couldn't allow him to live 9 more months?

Later I found out why.

My senior year in college, I was a Resident Assistant in a

freshman dorm,which was another thing I was not very happy with God about! Thankful for a job as a RA, I would have preferred to be in the junior/senior dorm with all my friends. Another why? Except for one lone transfer student, my good friend Eadie, the floor was entirely inhabited by freshman. In the first semester between September and Christmas break, 2 of the girls lost their fathers. God vividly provided the answer to my question - Why? And I now understood my story. Because of my experience I could be a listening ear to these young girls. I understood their pain, their loss, and could help as someone who had experienced the same set of circumstances.

While we may not always enjoy the journey walking the path God has laid out for us, those life events, painful or joyous, make us who we are. With the passing of my father, I had questions of why? Yet the pain I experienced, burying my father at such a young age gave me a perspective that helped others in a time in their lives when they asked the same question, why?

> *While we may not always enjoy the journey walking the path God has laid out for us, those life events, painful or joyous, make us who we are.*

Wherever your journey has taken you and will take you still, it is your journey, walked only by you, in your shoes. The fact that only you have this perspective makes you extraordinary.

Shoes tell us a lot

As a young girl, my daughter Grace did not own a pair of tennis shoes since elementary school except if they were required for gym! Tennis shoes, sneakers, running shoes, or athletic shoes of any kind were simply not made for Grace. Not that she isn't athletic! She qualified for the state swim meet as a sophomore in high school- top 16 in the state of Michigan in the 500-yard Freestyle and again in her senior year. Her choice in shoes has nothing to do with her athletic ability, it is more about her style.

One evening we were watching a TV show together, Jay, Grace and I. The plot was a throwback to the 40's and everyone was dressed in the style of the times. Grace adored the feminin-

9

ity and style of the women's clothing. In one memorable scene the star was driving a convertible, sporting a driving scarf. Grace decided she is going to bring those back in style!

Being a classic style girl, athletic shoes are just not her thing.

Our shoes tell us a lot about who we are.

Why Can't You Be More Like Your Sister?

I am the third of four children. My sister Sandy is the oldest, then comes brother Greg, me, and then the baby of the family, Tom. Per the Book Order book by Dr. Kevin Leman, my family is a classic example! Sandy, as the eldest, was the perfect child. Greg, as the second born is nothing like Sandy! I am the middle, and the most well balanced person (according to Dr. Leman's book!). Tom, the baby, got away with everything!

Growing up I constantly heard this phrase, " Why can't you be more like your sister?" My sister was and is a girly girl so to speak. She was a cheerleader in high school, had lots of boyfriends, would never go out of the house without makeup and she was gifted with my mother's extraordinary ability to sew anything!

I on the other hand was and still am more of a tomboy preferring softball and soccer. I have no problem going out of the house without makeup and cannot sit still long enough to sew a straight line! Mother just didn't know what to do with me so I heard that phrase frequently! As a result, I possess a very strong desire to be a unique individual, variant from the norm, definitely not ordinary. Totally extraordinary!

Where am I?

Moving from the ordinary life to the extraordinary life involves asking three questions. The first being "Who am I?", the second is, " Where am I?"

Look around. Right now, right where you are. Answer this question, where am I?

You may have answered: I am in 2016. I am In my house. I am In Michigan. I am a single mother. I am a wife. I am a student. You may have answered with the year, your physical location, your geographical location, your situation in life; all specific answers based on your current perspective!

I am here

While "masquerading as the ordinary is exhausting" is my life motto, another phrase that holds great importance to me is " I am here and this is now". Whatever your answer to the question, "Where am I?" , the above phrase is the truth. It doesn't matter how you answered, what matters is that you focus on the now - where you are on your journey today.

All too often we feel stuck and in a rut with where we are on our journey. We want to be someplace different. We want to live in a different house or state. We want to be married or to have children. We want to graduate and move onto our vocation already! We seem to always want to be somewhere further down the road on our journey. What we fail to realize is, where we are is exactly where we need to be at this point in time.

A popular phrase that I recall from college that is synonymous with this principle, " bloom where you are planted." Wherever you are in this life, or wherever you are at this moment in time, bloom. Learn from your present circumstances. Live in the moment, in this place. The things you experience in this phase of life will move you from the ordinary to the extraordinary.

Onto the next thing

When our son Torrey was born, I was elated! Our first-born was a boy, a five generation tradition! However, it was not too long before the novelty wore off. Not to sound harsh or selfish, but sleep deprivation, dirty diapers, and inconsolable newborn babies are not what I imagined about when I dreamt of having children!

I began to wonder when he would grow up and be out of diapers? Then when would he go to school? When would he be in high school? What year would he graduate and enter college? OH wait, no, come home don't go to college! When will he get married? He did! Now when will I have grandkids? (We are actu-

11

ally not allowed to ask that question for 7 years). But you get the picture! We spend so much time waiting for the next life event, that often we miss the current phase and what it holds for us today.

I am here and this is now. Live in the moment today. Are your kid's young? Enjoy them now! Get down on the floor and play with them, the dishes and laundry can wait! Do your teenagers have their eye roll perfected? Schedule movie nights or make dinner as a family. Start a conversation about what is important in their world today, rather than what chore they need to finish before dinner.

For empty nesters, the journey today is very different than it has been for many years. Drop everything and go on a date! You can! No one is home to be to shuttle to the next practice! I am looking forward to next year when Jay and I experience a change of course as Grace goes off to college! Initially this was a somber thought until I realized I can actually sleep in!

Ladies, in order to move from the ordinary to the extraordinary, we have to live right where we are, today. You are right where you need to be. Just as we can only wear one pair of shoes at a time, we can only live one moment at a time.

What am I becoming?

Back to the shoe closet. Who am I, Where am I, and What am I becoming? These 3 questions direct you to explore the core of who you are?

While spending some quiet time with my children, one of my favorite books to read as they were growing up was Dr. Seuss, Oh the Places You'll Go.

Congratulations! Today is your day. You're off to great
Places! You're off and away!
You have brains in your head.
You have feet in your shoes.
You can steer yourself any direction you choose.
You're on your own. And you know what you know.
And YOU are the decide you will decide where to go!

There are basically only two directions in life: chasing after God or running away from God. With brains in our heads and feet in our shoes, we steer ourselves in the direction we choose. Running away from God keeps us locked in the ordinary life. Chasing after God leads us His very presence where He wants us to experience the extraordinary life!

"For shoes, put on the peace that comes from the Good News so that you will be fully prepared." (Ephesians 6:15 NIV) Even the Bible talks about shoes! We have to be fully prepared for where God is calling us to go! We need to be ready for what He has for us! Just as you would want to choose the right shoes for an event or activity, God wants to use your experience in the here and now to prepare you for what He has in store for you next week, month, or year. What we are becoming? We are either becoming a woman who chases after God, thus extraordinary, or runs away from Him, staying in the ordinary. Which are you? What are you becoming?

A Lover of Shoes

While not a "fashionista", or a trendsetter, I definitely have always had a love affair with shoes! My flamboyant great aunt Nuce, short for Lucille, took me "back to school" shoe shopping when I was 6 in Tampa, FL at a landmark Macy's. Coming from Atlanta, GA, I was a big-city girl but at 6, this Macy's felt enormous! As we entered the shoe department, the aroma of all the new shoes was overwhelming- that clean leather smell! MMMMMM!

As we surveyed all the choices, my eyes zeroed in on THE pair. The only pair in the whole world for me - shiny patent leather Mary Jane's! The front of the shoe was shiny red and the back of the shoe was shiny blue. The strap was half blue and half red, with tiny white buttons. I fell immediately in love and had to have them! Mother tried to talk me out of them because these were supposed to be "back to school" shoes and she was not sure these were the most practical shoes for everyday wear. Aunt Nuce bought them and I put them on immediately! Walking around the rest of the day feeling like a Disney princess. To this day, I wish I had those shoes. No one else at my school had shoes like mine. As an adult, I loved those shoes because they were one of a kind among many! In Macy's with my Aunt Nuce was where my love of shoes began as well as my desire to be unique.

Fast-forward 17 years, to the first time I needed new dress shoes as a married woman. " Honey, is it in the budget for me to buy a new pair of shoes?" Jay's response, " Yes. The best solution would be to purchase a pair of black pumps that go with every-thing and are very practical." NOOOOOO! My new husband did not know me, Laura Laffoon, at all! I could not purchase shoes that would be like everyone else. That would be heretical and ruf-fle every fiber of who I am! I needed to have unique, extraordinary shoes!

While this book is not about buying the perfect pair of shoes, it is meant to explore how a God who loves you has creat-ed you for a specific purpose and a rewarding adventure only you can experience. This book will help you leave the ordinary life behind and live your life extraordinary! When we live the life God created us to live we live an extraordinary one.

No two women's shoe closets look exactly the same be-cause you have been passionately created in God's image. You have been intentionally made with a combination of passion and purpose. The shoes you have in your closet reflect who you are, your hobbies, your style, your comfort, your story.

Embrace the story of your life thus far and realize your individual experiences have made you who you are. Next, we are going to look at our journey, and where we are right now! Where our shoes are taking us? Which shoes help us run toward HIM, and the extraordinary life He created us to live!

> *Embrace the story of your life thus far and realize your individual experiences have made you who you are.*

Comfortable Shoes

Do you have friends that you cannot remember where you met or when you actually became friends? They seem to have always been there, as if there was no beginning to your friendship. These friends are like your most comfortable pair of shoes that sit by the back door and greet you when you come home from work each day. You slip your feet into them and experience that feeling of pure contentment and relaxation. Even if those shoes are ten years old and becoming worn out, the feeling when we put them on is beyond compare! We all have those friends that when we are together we can simply be ourselves - content and relaxed, glad to be together. These friendships span the years and even if we live miles apart, or right next door, when we are together time is not an issue, and we pick up right where we left off when we were last together.

I have several pair of "comfortable shoes"! I have friends from my childhood, friends from college, friends of 25+ years, and new friends, all whom allow me to be myself. Comfortable friendships allow you to live authentically.

Like a comfortable pair of shoes

I am pretty sure Cindy, Carrie, and I met in the crib nursery at North Avenue Presbyterian Church. We attended Sunday school together, sang in the Choir-Lights children's choir together, sat in church together, and even skipped church to go to Krispy Kreme Donut Shop together. We were always together.

We were the "three musketeers" until the summer before our freshman year in high school. We were headed to Jekyll Island, GA for a youth convention. On the bus we met Deaver. She had recently started attending our church. We found out almost immediately that we shared common interests. It was a great week in Jekyll Island and at the end of it Deaver became the "fourth musketeer" of our merry band of friends.

Though we all attended different high schools in Atlanta, GA, we spent many weekends together at one another's house and were in church together on Sundays.

One Saturday, we were spending the night at Deaver's house. We were enjoying a typical evening at a local mall: We ate at the food court, walked in and out of stores gazing at the lastest fashion, and thoroughly enjoyed just being together. We noticed that there were not a lot of people in the mall. So we thought it would be fun to just dip our toes into one of the mall fountains! Haven't you ever thought about it? You are walking through the mall, pass by the fountains, and it is as if they are calling you. Beckoning you with the crystal clear water, "come on in!". Well, we did! Harmless fun and we didn't get caught!

Growing up, getting married and starting families we moved to different corners of the country. We still keep in touch via Facebook and email. Several years ago a reunion in a rented a condo in St. Simons Island, GA, found us laughing hysterically, listening to "our" music, reminiscing and catching up on many years of life. One day we decided to take a bike ride and had great fun exploring the island together. That evening involved biking into town for ice cream at Dairy Queen, and seeing who could fit their ice cream cone into their mouth all at once....I won!

We may have grown up and moved away from each other but friendships like these never fade.

When I attended the funeral of my step-dad a year or so ago, I was back in my old stomping grounds, at North Avenue Presbyterian church. My child-hood friend, Cindy, attended the funeral. We got to spend an hour catching up on each other's lives, chatting about old times. Even though it had been years since we had been together, it was as if we had just seen each other yesterday. It was like slipping on a comfortable pair of shoes.

I have a great respect and love for these three ladies, Cindy, Carrie, and Deaver, who have been a part of shaping and forming who I am today. The memories we made, the antics we found ourselves in, and the time we spent growing up together will always be a part of me.

We have our friendships from childhood, but life goes on, we grow up and move away, we develop other friendships that also contribute to who we are and what we are becoming.

When it comes to these type of friendships, those like comfortable shoes, develop those that allow you to let your hair down and do life together. I believe there are three different types of friendships we need to pursue and develop in our lives: friendships that make us better, friendships that strengthen us, and friendships that tell us the truth.

Friendships that makes you better

When Jay and I moved to Alma, MI in 1987, I left my hometown, my lifelong friends, my entire family and started a new adventure! We moved here knowing not a soul!

We were brought to Michigan to start a Youth For Christ (YFC) chapter in the central Michigan area. We were constantly meeting people, teenagers, school administrators, but not really developing friendships.

One of first partnerships in this new ministry was a community center run by a local church. This community center, His Place, ran a ministry for elementary aged children. The staff was finding that after the children finished their program and moved onto middle school there was nothing for them. As a result a group of people in the community contacted YFC to start a chapter in the central Michigan area. Our goal was to provide something for the middle school and high school aged young people in our community.

I began working alongside the people at His Place. The center offers free exercise classes, sports leagues, summer camps, and after-school programs for youth. I volunteered in the elementary program so I could become familiar with the kids and families of the community. I volunteered in any way necessary to catch a vision for this ministry and how we could enhance it for these kids entering their teenage years.

It was at His Place that I developed my first real friendship in Michigan. Working alongside Joneen, she and I discovered that we had a lot in common. We both lost our fathers as teenagers. We are both fun loving, love to shop, to eat and read! We both like exercising (notice I used like not love). We are both passionate about ministry. We became fast friends. Joneen Wight became a friend that made me a better person.

When Joneen and I met, I was 25 years old, and only 3 years married. Joneen was 40 and had been married 22 years. I began to observe the attraction between her and her husband, Russ. They were still very much in love with each other. Joneen and Russ were also very much a team. They lived their life together always as partners, making decisions together.

As our friendship grew, I began to learn from Joneen what it meant to be a Godly wife and woman.

She taught me to make my husband my priority.

Joneen made Russ breakfast, lunch and dinner...everyday! What? Jay made his own breakfast, we went out for lunch, and we figured out dinner as the day progressed!

Joneen ironed all Russ' clothes. I didn't believe in ironing. I believe wrinkles give clothes character! Jay did his own ironing.

As for sex, well, I did say she made her husband her priority!

As I watched, I realized that I could learn a lot about marriage and loving my husband from Joneen. They had the type of marriage I wanted. They loved each other unconditionally and were each other's priority. They were more than lovers, they were partners in life.

My friendship with Joneen made me a better wife.

I watched how she dealt with people. She never lost her temper with those who could be hard to live with. She always granted grace and tried to see the best in people. When parents were an hour late in picking up their children from His Place, she always made sure everything was okay with the parents.

I watch how she cared for those in need. Her home and office were always open to those who needed a listening ear, money to pay a bill, or a place to stay.

My friendship with Joneen made me a better person.

People in our lives need to make us a better person. Friendships add value to the person that we are, and the person we are becoming. We need to surround ourselves with people who make us better and whom we can make better as well.

If you were to ask Joneen how I have helped her become a better person, she would probably say I have helped her to stand up for herself and not let people run all over her. She is a person who would say yes to every good thing that comes along. She would wear herself out, and her family. She has become a person who tries to say yes to what is most important, and no to those that are good but less important.

Friendships need to make each person a better human being.

> *Friendships need to make each person a better human being.*

Friendships that strengthen you

Tiff and I met as a result of Jay and I working on staff at a local church. Tiff's husband, Brad, was on staff as well and we worked alongside him in ministry. A year into our time at the church, through a series of circumstances, the four of us began to get-together every month or so just to discuss life and such. Brad and Tiff are much younger than Jay and I, and were going through some crisis'. Jay and I felt the need and desire to walk alongside them through this time.

While our initial intent was to help Tiff and Brad with the stress and frustration they were going through, the opposite happened as well. Brad and Tiff helped Jay and I in some difficulties we were experiencing. I soon found out that Tiff was a friend that spiritually challenged me and ultimately strengthened me.

Tiff is a prayer warrior and has an unbelievable faith in Jesus that spills over into those around her. She has challenged my beliefs ,my doubts, my fears and helped me in my faith.

Our daughter Grace was experiencing some symptoms physically that no one could really diagnose. Jay and I felt we needed to have the elders of our church pray for her. We asked Brad and Tiff to pray with us as well. After about 15 minutes of prayer, the Elders needed to get back to the worship service. Tiff insisted we stay and pray further. We did, for about another 30 minutes. Tiff would pray and then ask Grace how she was feeling. When Grace would respond with the symptoms still felt abnormal, then Tiff would pray for that specifically. As I watched and listened to Tiff pray, I remembered when I was that persistent and tenacious in my prayer life. It had been too long since I had fervently prayed for the Lord to answer.

My friendship with Tiff has strengthened and renewed me spiritually.

Friendships that tell you the truth

If you are married and have a mother in law, you have a person in your life that tells you the truth! At least my mother in law does! I can always count on Doyce to give me a truthful answer, and at times more truthful than I really desired.

Seriously though, sometimes friendships that tell you the truth are the hardest to grow and cultivate. It is easy to be truthful when the truth is something someone wants to hear. It isn't so easy to be truthful when the truth hurts. We can have the best of friends but when it comes to being truthful with each other, we find it hard to do.

True authentic friends are ones that can tell each other the truth in all circumstances.

Joneen and I love to shop together. We make Christmas shopping dates, birthday shopping dates, and no reason shopping dates. Shopping is one of our favorite pastimes!

I am in the fitting room trying on an outfit and need her opinion.
I would try on an outfit and ask her what she thought and I could see the visible struggle she would have telling me the outfit just wasnt the right fit.

Inevitably after a shopping day with Joneen, I would go home, try on my new clothes for Jay, and he would comment, "

Joneen let you buy that! I thought she was your friend!" Joneen is one of the most genuinely nice people in the world and she had a very difficult time telling me when something did not look very good on me! I finally convinced her, after 25 years, that I want her honesty!

We all need people in our lives that can be truthful whether the news is good or bad.

The problem with friendships

Friendships are one of the most important parts of our human existence, yet our culture causes us to keep people at arm's length. We have many modern conveniences but those conveniences become detrimental to our relationships. We can turn on our air-conditioners and close ourselves inside our homes, never seeing our neighbors.

Two summers ago we invited our next-door neighbors, Luke and Martha, over for dinner. This was the first time we had dinner together even though we had lived next door for 16 years. It was a great evening and we had a wonderful time together. We joked that when winter rolls around, we can look forward to seeing each other again next summer. Why? Because we close ourselves in our homes, cut off from neighbors, much more in the winter months in Michigan versus those summer months.

In spite of modern conveniences, we need to be aware of building friendships.

We live in a very mobile environment. Gone are the days of family homesteads where generations stayed in one place and worked the family farm or business. On average as adults we will move 3-4 times in our lifetime. This makes seeking, building, and maintaining new friendships difficult.

I was speaking to a young mother who shared how she and her husband have moved 4 times in their ten years of married life. As a result it is hard for her to make friends, because she is afraid to become attached and then leave. It is too painful.

Mobility is a great thing. We can travel to places we never thought possible. See things many of our grandparents only read about. However, it can be detrimental to building lasting friend-ships that has humans we so desperately crave.

We live in a culture controlled by technology. With the invention of cell phones, we can decide with whom we want to talk to, and when we want to talk to them.

Jay and I were watching college football in the family room. Shortly after Grace had gone upstairs to her room our home phone rings. I check the caller id to make sure it isn't a solicitor only to see that it is Grace's cell phone. "Our daughter is calling us from her bedroom." I picked up the home phone, and say to Grace, "I can't believe that you are calling me from upstairs!" She replied, "Well you should thank me, mom, because I didn't call your cell phone and make you get out of your chair to answer my question."

Cell phones and social media have contributed to the friendship void in our lives. Facebook makes us think we have many friends. Between our Jay and Laura page, and my personal page, I have over 8,000 friends. The sad reality is most of those "friends" I have never really spent any quality time with developing a friendship.

Often we hide behind technology and ordinary modern conveniences. People are starving for someone to listen and care about them. To let them know they are loved and not alone. While they are a unique creative individual, what they are experiencing may be something you have experienced in another stage of life. Being extraordinary means moving beyond this and developing face to face friendships that make you better, strengthen you and create an honest environment.

Five Friends

As we wrap up this chapter, I want you to think of your five closest friends. Write down their names then beside each name write down whether they make you better, strengthen you, or tell you the truth. If one of these friendships is not evident in your life, then go out and purposefully find someone who can be that type of friend. We were created to be relational, to have true friends, and not just Facebook friends but friends that allow us to kick off our shoes, let our hair down and live life together!

Fitness Shoes

Exercise (ek-ser-shayz) verb: to put into action, practice, or use

As a child, your playtime is spent running around with friends outdoor games, jumping on a trampoline, skating, riding scooters, or enjoying the popular game of the day. As a child you never saw this as exercise, you were simply playing!

As we age, our fun time is replaced by other priorities. As adults, we have to make a conscious decision to carve out time in our weekly schedule to exercise, as it no longer feels like play! Doctors tell us that we must challenge our muscles for the benefit of our heart and health. I prefer the carefree playtime of a child over working out on P90X, completing a Crossfit routine , or simply jogging!

"Don't you realize that your body is the temple of the Holy Spirit, who lives in you and was given to you by God? You do not belong to yourself, for God bought you with a high price. So you must honor God with your body." 1 Corinthians 6:19-20 (NLT)

Honoring God with our body moves us past the ordinary and makes us extraordinary. Basically there are 5 areas of our lives that we need to keep healthy: mental, social, physical, emotional, and spiritual. These 5 areas are part of the temple, the body, and when we keep it all healthy and running well, we can honor God.

The Mental Area

At the end of a very productive day of writing my mind is toast, mush, gone. At the end of a very mentally exhausting day, I either want a nap or to read a very un- thought provoking book. I really just want to relax!

So often though, as women, our minds can think of many other things we can be doing other than relaxing. The list is endless. We feel guilty if we take time for ourselves to reflect, rejuvenate, and recharge. Yet taking care of our mental health involves taking time for our minds to turn off and relax.

> *We feel guilty if we take time for ourselves to reflect, rejuvenate, and recharge.*

My challenge to you would be this, whether it is dishes, laundry, working or something else; whatever keeps you from taking time for yourself because you think it has to be done, do this. The next time that guilty thought comes into your subconscious, the one that says, " I can't relax, I have way too much to do", replace it with a thought of a way you can relax- sit and read, yoga, draw, take a walk. Be purposeful in your relaxing.

Some of you are like my friend Angie, who would say she couldn't possibly relax knowing the dirty dishes are in the sink! They must be done! The truth is, ladies, we have to give ourselves permission not to worry about those dirty dishes! Rather we need to take time to relax our brains and our bodies in order to stay healthy!

While the chores won't go away, give yourself a mental break from caring for everyone else to concentrate on your health. Finding a source of stress relief will help you be better prepared for life's surprises.

Mommy Porn

There can be many avenues to relaxation. Some are better than others and some should be used in small doses.

Soap Operas were a huge deal when I was growing up. My mom and sister watched *All My Children*. In college, *Luke and Laura*, from *General Hospital*, were all the rage, I can remember people scheduled their classes around the broadcast time of *General Hospital*. In my mind's eye, I can clearly see the day *Luke and Laura* were married. The living area of my dorm was packed with guys and girls watching the main event! Many of them skipped class! I couldn't believe it.

TV can be a great avenue for relaxation. We can DVR a show to watch at our convenience. With the onset of Amazon Video Streaming and Netflix, we never have to miss an episode of

" our show".

While I would still say I'm still not into soap operas, my husband, Jay, would not agree! An avid fan, of Downton Abbey, 24, and Scandal, my viewing time on the treadmill doesn't take away from family time, so in my opinion it works. It is a way for me to turn off my brain from work and chores and lose myself in the show.

There were times I would watch 24, that Jay got a bit jealous. I was watching it when I exercised, and that was okay. At night when we would relax and read a book, or do non-work related computer stuff, I would watch the next episode. When traveling, I would waste time in the airport watching the next episode. 24 did become an obsession. I did take a break from it. True confessions!

Purposeful and mindful relaxation is good for our mental health.

Facebook, Wanelo, Pinterest, and the plethora of social media is another way to turn off our brain but can also be an avenue of relaxation that should used in small doses. I simply love to sit down and open Pinterest, search for recipes and DIY projects, but there are times that before I know it hours have passed, I am passed relaxing and have moved onto time wasting!

Imagine this. Take a day, week or even a month of social media fasting! No Facebook, Pinterest, or any other social media outlet for the time you choose. Ask yourself these questions, " Do I miss it"? " Am I experiencing withdrawal?" " Do I snap at my family because I'm out of touch with what is happening on Facebook? We must be mindful of how we relax and how it affects those around us when we move past relaxing to obsession.

Do you love me more than your book?

As a child I grew up reading in bed to relax before bedtime. When my parents didn't allow it, I would take a flashlight to bed and read under the covers! Reading became a part of my natural bedtime routine.

When I was first married, reading was still a part of my bedtime routine. When we would go to bed, I would turn on the bedside table lamp, kiss Jay goodnight, and read. I was oblivious to the fact that this bothered him. It never crossed my mind that I should put my book down, let alone, not even bring it into the bedroom!

One summer night, after I kissed Jay goodnight, he did that deep sigh thing, sat up and looked me in the eye and asked' "Do you love me more than your book?" Taken aback, I became a bit defensive, responding, " Of course I don't! What a silly question!" Then he began to share that reading a book in bed every night made him feel inadequate. It hurts his feelings that I wanted my book more than it appeared I wanted him.

Reading is still very relaxing for me but I now do it at a time that doesn't communicate to my husband that it is more important than him. At times, our shows, our social media, and our books or magazines, can cause us to live in an alternate reality and ignore the real people who are most important to us.

> *At times, our shows, our social media, and our books or magazines, can cause us to live in an alternate reality and ignore the real people who are most important to us.*

Honoring God in this mental area means giving ourselves permission to relax and turn off our brains but also balancing that with life and family. Taking care of our mental health is what moves us from ordinary to extraordinary.

The Social Area

One would think that people who stand on a stage and speak to others, for a living, are extroverts. However that is not always true.

Whether you are an introvert or extrovert isn't whether you are talkative or outgoing, shy or quiet. While these are definite commonalities among these personality types, the real basis for deciding whether you are an introvert or extrovert is based on how you answer this question, "What rechargers me?"

As an example when Jay used to travel alone, he would come home from a weekend of speaking in need of some peace and quiet. After a couple of hours of "Jay Time", he was refreshed and ready to re-engage with the kids and I.

While his gift is speaking, which involves being with people on a regular basis for long periods of time, he is an introvert. He needs time alone to recharge.

In order to stay healthy socially, we have to do life with other people - easier said than done for an introvert. Most introverts would prefer doing life with small gatherings of trusted friends and an extrovert would be delighted to do life with a party of people!

The reality is that we need other people in our lives. We can't exist without deep connections with others. So whether you are an introvert or an extrovert, find people you can do life with. Find an intimate group or community you can be a part of. Deep interaction with people is vital to help us realize that we are not alone in our fears, frustrations, and irrational thoughts!

> *The reality is that we need other people in our lives.*

The reality is that finding those deep connections is more difficult today in the world we live than maybe it used to be. When families lived closer, and one income could support an entire family, men and women gathered separately to discuss their lives and growing families. The older family members were able to share concerns and experiences with the younger members, through each phase of life. Today's families are more isolated and mentors are found in friends rather than family members. Trust and loyalty no longer come naturally but take longer to develop and build.

Deep connections don't happen overnight. It takes time, sometimes years to build that trust and honesty that are the foundation for a community of people doing life together. Jay and I have been a part of a small group of couples for 20 years. The connection didn't just happen but has taken years of building relationships with these couples. We get together every week to talk about life, share joys and struggles, and how we can support each other.

I am not suggesting you to go out every night to be with

people. For introverts that would be physically, emotionally, and mentally exhausting. I am challenging you to do life with people on a regular basis, whether that is once a week or once a month.

Admittedly, as we have begun to travel more, I am becoming more of an introvert. Life's circumstances mold you and change you. Some weeks, it would be very easy for Jay and I too look at each other and decide to be socially isolated for a very long time!

We experienced a revelation when we found ourselves trying to talk our daughter Grace out of being actively involved in social events. We came to the conclusion we needed to encourage not discourage her to do life with other people.

Being a part of a community, living life with others not only gives us a support system but honors our Creator who designed us to be in relationship with others.

The Physical Area

Several years ago, Jay and I decided to get serious about impacting our physical health. We joined a local college recreation center and thought that laying out money would motivate us to go out and exercise. It did at first but then it just got boring!

We moved on and found a program " Body for Life", which is an eating and exercise program that we could do at home The eating part of the program involved balancing your carbs and proteins, while eating 6 small meals a day. This was doable in the Laffoon house.

The exercise portion of Body for Life was a little more challenging! The basics involved exercising 6 days a week: 3 days of strength training and 3 days of cardio training which initially doesn't sound difficult. However the premise of the exercise program is that no matter what you are doing on any given day (cardio or strength training) you must exercise to the point that you feel as if you will die.

In the first 6 months, we tackled it with determination! On any given day that I would do strength training to the point that I thought I would die, I could not accomplish anything worthwhile the rest of the day! Showering was an effort as I couldn't lift my arms above my head to wash my hair!

As a resourceful person, I devised a way to wash my hair on strength-training days. I purchased a soap on a rope, cut off the rope and tied it to my shampoo bottle, suspending it from the shower head until it was even with my head.

After an exhausting workout, I would wet my hair and then bang my head on the shampoo bottle until the shampoo oozed out onto the wall. I would rub my head against the wall until I felt my head was scrubbed and then rinse!

We do many crazy antics just to stay healthy! Being physically healthy means taking of your physical body thru proper nutrition, exercise, and sleep.

Your body is eating itself!

Words that strike fear in a mother, when they are spoken about your child's body!

When Grace was in 7th grade she pursued her love and began swimming competitively. It was as though she had been born to swim as she is tall and has very broad shoulders.

As a high school sophomore, she qualified in the 500 free-style event for the state meet and was in the top 16 in our state in her event. That summer, her coach told her she could break any record on the board at the pool.

At the same time, she had begun experiencing pain in her back, ribs, and shoulders. She had experienced these pains before, but not to the same intensity. We attributed all the pain to the intense training she was doing for the conference meet.

Soon it became very clear that this was not just sore muscles. There were days that she would come home from swim practice and lay on the couch and cry for the rest of the evening because it was too painful to move. She walked like she was 80 years old as opposed to 15.

After 9 long months of pain and questioning, and missing her entire junior season, we found a holistic medical doctor that figured out what was wrong. The short version is that she was severely anemic and the protein she was consuming was not being absorbed into her muscles. As a result the body began to burn her muscle and her joints connective tissue for fuel and release a chemical that caused temporary juvenile arthritis, thus the pain. All the doctor did was change her eating habits and put her on vitamins!

Being physically healthy is not about being thin, it is about taking care of the body you have been given to the best of your ability. The importance of eating healthy became very clear to us. Our daughter has returned to the lovely, funny, and precocious person she was before the pain controlled her life.

The more you move the better you feel

We were created to move! We have two arms and two legs, and one bottom. I think that means we should move 4 times as much as we sit!

I am not saying you should go out and run a marathon tomorrow. I am not even saying you need to follow an exercise program. What I am saying is you need to move daily. Take the stairs not the elevator, walk your neighborhood, ride a bike when you can instead of driving.

My mother is 84 years old and gets out everyday just so she moves. My in-laws are 77 and 79, and they walk a mile everyday! There is no excuse not to move!

Exercise is good for us physically but it can also be a mental release. Sometimes I do my best creating on my morning run. Moving gets every part of your physical body in sync with the rest of you.

I am a sleeper!

I love sleep! I always have. In high school, I developed a

habit of coming home right after school and taking a 30-minute nap. The nap would refresh me and allow me to focus on home-work and chores.

It is common knowledge that the average adult should get 8 hours of sleep a night. The reality is adults average 6 hours a night. That short amount is unhealthy and not productive sleep. Sleep is our downtime. It is when our bodies and minds can shut down, repair and rejuvenate. When we don't allow our bodies and minds this downtime, we are cheating ourselves out of our health.

After a long travel weekend, I am a stickler for sleeping late on Monday morning. Jay used to balk at this concept, as he felt he needed to get in the office first thing in order to wrap up travel expenses, answer email and other details from the weekend. I insisted that for his health physically and emotionally, he needed to stay in bed for a bit longer. He conceded and has experienced the benefits. Now, on occasion, I even catch him napping!

Proper nutrition, exercise and plenty of sleep are what will keep us physically healthy. Moving from ordinary to extraordinary means taking care of our physical bodies.

The Emotional Area

Figuring out our emotions as women is a never-ending process, isn't it? Some days we are just annoyed by any one, one word and everyone, and we can't explain why!

" Another word and you die!"

Jay and I run everyday that it is possible. The other day we went out for our run. During our warm up – which is basically a mile walk- I was having a talk with myself. That morning as I was making breakfast, Jay made a comment that annoyed me! I had literally just placed the meat in the pan to brown, and Jay, in a bossy yet sing song voice says from the other room, " I don't hear anything sizzling in there yet." I became very annoyed. I replied, " Well you must be deaf than because it is cooking."

As we left for our run, I was still annoyed, even though it was 2 hours later! As we walked, he glanced over, and asked me why I had a scowl on my face (this is where I was having a talk to myself about being annoyed). I replied with a bit of a grunt. He kept talking. The more words that came out of his mouth, the more annoyed I became. After a few more minutes, Jay asked, " Are you mad at me?" I replied, " I am not sure why, but I am very annoyed with you! And if you say another word, you might have to die!" He laughed. Death did not ensue, lucky for him!

He makes comments all the time and I don't usually let it ruin my demeanor but find a sarcastic way to let him know the impact of his words. Yes, sarcasm is one of my spiritual gifts. But this day was different, I was very annoyed, and really could not find a good reason as to why his words hit a nerve. This is often the emotional rollercoaster we find ourselves on.

When it comes to being emotionally healthy we need to take two actions: 1) be aware of the difference between your perception and reality and 2) let it out!

We had been married 25 years, before I figured out that Jay could detect my emotional state better than I could! Ladies, we all understand that there are *certain times* we are more emotional than others. My *certain time* has always been just prior to the beginning of my cycle. Jay could always predict the date of "my visitor" to the day, which would annoy me greatly! He would always say he could tell based on my reactions yet I never believed it was due to my emotional state.

As our daughter entered that time in her life, the pattern was so evident! She was not a very pleasant person the week before! When I began to pay attention, becoming more aware of my own emotions, I realized he was right! I had a period of time (no pun intended) right before "my visitor" that I was noticeably crankier than other times!

Realizing this, I began to be prepared for the onslaught of emotions that would overcome me and find stress outlets to handle them rationally! I also admitted to my husband that he was right! Humility is always good.

Becoming aware does not replace the need to express our emotions! A good cry is very therapeutic! Holding our frustrations inside is detrimental to our health. The key is expressing our true

feelings without hurting other people, and/or damaging relationships.

When my children were younger, I held my reaction to a
minor infraction to the "count of 10". In theory this would allow
me time to respond in a manner that was not spiteful yelling that
would crush their spirit.

This isn't always a fail-proof plan especially when you feel
as if you are having an out of body experience, watching yourself
screaming and yelling, not even believing that it is you! Even the
day, I told Jay that if he said another word, he might die, I realized that he was annoying me, for no reason other than his mere
existence! I spoke these words to him very calmly, so calmly that it
became laughable.

Awareness of emotions, and expressing them in a way
that isn't hurtful or damaging, becomes very healthy for us as
individuals. But this doesn't occur without clear communication.
Female emotional outburst are something many men have difficulty enduring as there is no quick fix; there is nothing they can "do",
so they tune out. I challenge you to find ways to keep the communication gateway open. If any negative outburst occurs, you be the
one to explain how you really feel in a calmer setting. His reaction
may surprise you! In doing this you will move from ordinary to
extraordinary.

The Spiritual Area

All too often we focus on the spiritual area as the only way
we can honor God. Is this area important? Absolutely. Yet it is only
one part of the whole that makes up who we are as a person.

"UMM, No Steve I won't pray!"

Jay and I have been involved with Compassion International a child sponsorship organization for over 15 years. Compassion
exists to meet the unique spiritual, social, physical, and economic
needs of children trapped in poverty.

I had been speaking on behalf of Compassion for 5 years before I ever experienced real poverty.

When we landed in Rio de Janeiro, Brazil, I experienced unforgettable fear, trepidation, and excitement. This was my first trip out of the continental United States, as well as my first trip with Compassion. Our schedule included a few days of sightseeing in Rio, then spending a few days visiting Compassion Projects all over the country of Brazil.

As we were flying to Fortaleza, the 5th largest city, located in the northeastern part of Brazil, we had a stop over in Recife, known as the Brazilian Venice. During our long layover, we were given the opportunity to visit a Compassion Project in Recife.

Recife is located on the coast of northeastern Brazil and at the confluence to two rivers. Crossing a tenuous handmade bridge, we journeyed to the Compassion project, located along water's edge. Along the shoreline were shacks we could see right through!

After visiting the Compassion center, we ventured into some of the children's homes in the project. As we stood in the doorway of the home, on the water's edge, the mother explained to us in Spanish through an interpreter that because the floor of their house was nothing but slats through which water was visible that when the tide came in the water came up through the floor bringing trash and waste. When the water went back out again, most often the trash remained. The mother explained that she tried to get the children's beds up off the floor so the beds didn't get wet and soiled. The desperate scene was all too common on the island. Most heart wrenching for me was the view of the million dollar condos just across the water from the island.

Needless to say as heart took in the scene around me, I became angry we would allow this to happen as Christians. I was angry at the people living in the million dollar condos who looked at these shacks every day. I was angry at God that people lived like this.

As we were saying goodbye to the mother, Steve, our Compassion staff person, asked me if I would pray. I replied with a resounding no as I was too angry and heart-broken. When

34

Steve respectfully asked again and again I replied no. Tears were streaming down my face as Steve prayed.

Life has not been the same since my first experience with real poverty. As a result I have become a staunch supporter of Compassion International! Freeing children from poverty in Jesus' name is much bigger than my small world in Alma, MI when it seems like a small crisis the cable service is interrupted and the TV and internet are not functional!

Maintaining our spiritual health is more than attending church, giving of our tithe, and being involved with a life group. We move from ordinary to extraordinary, when we understand that what we profess to believe needs to be put into action. Whether serving in a local soup kitchen or traveling to a third world country to minister to others, faith without works is indeed dead.

15 Minutes

We encourage married people to practice 5 different healthy habits for their marriage. One habit is to have 15 minutes of uninterrupted conversation with each other every day. Before the kids get up, after they go to bed, over lunch - when it occurs isn't as important as being committed to setting aside the time as a priority. Our calendars and To Do Lists are full of activities and tasks. But ask yourself, " What is more important that your relationship with your spouse?" Uninterrupted conversation, face to face, on a daily basis for 15 minutes builds a connection between husband and wife on many levels.

Your relationship with God isn't any different. We need that time with our Creator to connect with Him, listen to Him and He to us, and grow the relationship.

> *Your relationship with God isn't any different.*

Can you spend 15 minutes of uninterrupted conversation with God?

We all use the excuse of not having enough time in our day. Our time with God should priority number 1 in the planning of our day. When I take the time first thing in the morning, to spend time reading and praying, my day feels smoother. My focus is different. I am usually more productive and creative after spending time alone with God.

15 minutes feels so impractical! You may start your day with young children that need feeding and dressing and entertaining! Finding 15 minutes is like searching for a needle in a haystack. It doesn't have to be first thing in the morning but try taking the time right after they leave for school. If they aren't in school yet, try nap time. The important thing isn't when but rather doing it.

For many of us 15 minutes feels like eternity! " I have so many other things to get done in a day"! When my friend sits down to be quiet, read read and pray, her mind wanders to her to do list for the day. This is true for many of us. If that is you, try journaling, so your mind stays focused on what God used today to speak to your heart.

Getting started is the hardest part of any new habit. My recommendation is the Youversion app that includes the Bible, daily verses, different study plans. None of which requires more than 15 minutes to complete.

WE are so much more than physical

In a world, that emphasizes our physical form we need to understand that we are so much more. Being healthy is so much more than the food we consume and achieving the next level of the latest exercise trend.

We must be healthy mentally, socially, emotionally, and spiritually as well as physically.

As you read this statement you probably had a thought for how you can improve each of these areas in your own life. Write it down. Set a goal. Make a plan. Decide how to measure the achievement. Think of ways to maintain your health in each area.

The simple act of writing the words on paper imprints the idea in our mind. It doesn't mean we will always attain the goal we set but it is the beginning of acknowledging the need to improve our lifestyle and move from ordinary to extraordinary!

36

Recreation Shoes

There are nights when I fall into the bed and just wish I could do this day over. The chores aren't done. I didn't respond to my kids with love in certain situations. I didn't sit with my husband and just talk today. A do-over would fix that.

By bedtime, today is gone, over and done with, however with the dawn of a new day we get a fresh start. Too often we spend way too much time looking back. Have you ever been walking, glanced behind you and walked right into something? J.R.R. Tolkien wrote, " I will not walk backward in life".

> *J.R.R. Tolkien wrote, " I will not walk backward in life".*

It reminds me of visiting colleges with our daughter Grace during her last year of high school.

The visitation day always started with donuts, coffee and many free items with the college's logo such as bracelets, bags, pens, pencils, etc. Walking tours were an important part of each day. In groups of about ten students and parents we toured the campus with a guide who provided pertinent information concerning the college.

Our guide always walked backwards and talked, he was continually looking over his shoulder to make sure he wasn't running into another guide, or a wall, or a door. He would look over his shoulder, and continue to talk and we would lose what he was saying. It was actually comical at times, he would be walking backwards and talking and we could see what was coming that he couldn't and I found myself waiting to see if he would run into something! I am kind of twisted that way.

These observations cemented in my mind that what Tolkien said is true; we cannot walk backward in this life. We have to always move forward, each day start fresh, or we will lose sight of where we are going. If we are constantly living this life looking back to the "good old days" we will miss out on the days ahead, or worse yet, today!

"Brothers and sisters, I do not consider myself yet to have taken hold of it. But one thing I do: forgetting what is behind and straining toward what is ahead, I press on toward the goal to win the prize for which God has called me heavenward in Christ Jesus." Philippians 3:13-14 NIV

We were created to keep moving forward, to strive for what is ahead. We are to forget what is behind us, quit looking backwards. Don't waste your time dwelling on things of the past. The circumstances of the past have shaped who you are today but tomorrow is a new adventure!

"Let your eyes look straight ahead; fix your gaze directly before you. Give careful thought to the paths for your feet and be steadfast in all your ways." Proverbs 4:25-26 NIV

Each morning that you wake up is a new start, a new day to re-create who you are. How do we keep moving forward? How do we quit looking backward? We re-create our strength, our sanity, and our spirit. We do this by focusing on Jesus, eliminating busyness, and praying continuously.

Re-create your sanity

Focus, click, and shoot

I am a gadget girl. I love a new gadget. The coolest new one I purchased is a set of three lenses to add to my iPhone to enhance video and photo shooting! Oh my word, is it cool!

Reflecting on the all the cameras I have acquired over the years is nostalgic. First a Polaroid instamatic camera that gave you the picture immediately out a slot on the bottom of the camera. You had to wait for it to develop fully but it was still cool. The age of smaller cameras resulted in waiting for a store to be develop the pictures but the portable size was convenient.

The digital age made cameras very cool. When our daughter began participating in high school sports, I purchased a Nikon camera with an SD card which was the coolest thing ever! I could insert the card into my computer and have all her pics. When I received my new gadget, the iPad, I could use the adapter to store pics on the iPad OR just take pics with the iPad!

Technology has really changed our world, but through it all every camera still has to be focused. Whether it is a DSLR, an iPhone, or and iPad, in order to capture the best picture and achieve the best quality, you still have to focus on the subject.

In order for us to see the best picture of who we are, the clearest picture, we have to focus on Jesus. We lose our sanity when we take our eyes off of the One who created us and focus on ourselves, others, or the world around us.

Theodore Roosevelt said, "Comparison is the thief of joy." We lose our joy, thus our sanity, when we compare the life we live now to the good ol days, compare the gifts of others to what we see lacking in ourselves, and compare our wants and dreams to what we perceive as another's reality.

The power of focus

Do you know why you can stare at a light bulb that is on and not damage your eye but if you stare at a laser pointer, it causes damage to your eye? It is because of the power of focus. The laser pointer is focused energy as opposed to the 60 watt diffused light of a light bulb.

When we focus on Jesus, not only do we get a clearer picture of whom we are but we also have more power.

So what does focusing on Jesus look like?

One of my favorite verses of the Bible is found in Proverbs, "Charm is deceptive, and beauty is fleeting; but a woman who fears the Lord is to be praised."(Proverbs 31:30 NIV)

I would say for most women this is a comforting verse to read! I can tell you, and my husband will agree, I am not always the most charming person! I am comforted by the beginning of this verse in light of that fact. Concerning the beauty is fleeting? Well, I have told Jay time and time again, that he would be cranky too if his eyelashes were falling off and attaching themselves to his chin! Seriously, though, we all know we do not look like we did when we were 16. For some of us that is depressing and others it is encouraging. For all of us, we will age, we will sag, we will wrinkle.

How we focus on Jesus is found in the last phrase of this verse, "the fear of the Lord is to be praised". This fear is not founded in horror or terror; rather it is founded in awe and wonder. In order to focus on Jesus, we have to have a child like wonder of who He is. We have to put our eyes on Him as opposed to whatever might be happening in our lives.

Expectation and Excitement

The ability to focus on Jesus rather than what is happening around us, and or whatever circumstances we may find ourselves in, is easier said than done at times. I believe I have said before my husband and I run a marriage ministry. It is a non-profit 501 C 3. Which means we run the ministry on donations from other people and honorariums we are given for our events. At times, this is a real leap of faith. This fall we found ourselves with only one event a month! I will tell you that that is not enough events to run the ministry and pay our staff. It would be easy to focus on the lack of money and events we had, but I said to Jay, " I am going to expect the Lord to work and be excited to see what He is going to do!" And I was... for a day!

The day after I spoke those words to Jay, I got a reminder from al local youth ministry that I had volunteered to bring snack next week, and that snack needed to feed 150 teenagers! YIKES! My first reaction was to call the youth ministry and tell them we would have to pass this time because we couldn't afford to do the snack. But the Lord, as He so gently does, reminded me that I was focusing on Him and not our finances. He reminded me that I was expecting Him to work, so be faithful and let Him work.

Jay and I headed out to our local grocery store to purchase the snack and beverage. Thankfully our grocery store was running a 10 for $10 deal on Chex Mix! We picked up 20 bags. We also picked up 4 lemonade drink mixes that we 2 for $3. When we walked up to the self-checkout, we had our own groceries as

40

well, so Jay asked that I run the snacks through first so he could bag them separately. I had digital coupons that the computer asked if I wanted to use and I accepted without really paying much attention. As I finished running the snacks through the scanner, I glanced at the computer screen to see what the total cost of the snacks were...the total was at 0.00! Apparently the digital coupons I had totally covered the cost of the snacks for the youth ministry. Funny how that happened! Focusing on Jesus means just that we focus Him rather than our circumstances!

I don't go crazy

Pinterest is something to which I could very easily become addicted! It is my go to place for recipes, party ideas, gifts, etc. I also just love perusing it for creative and inspirational sayings. One of my favorites is "Aunty Acid". I just find these sayings hilarious! I read one recently that is never been truer for me, I just don't always want to admit it!

" *I don't go crazy. I am crazy. I just go normal from time to time.*"

I don't know if you ever feel like you are going insane but I do! When I walk into a room and can't remember why I went into it in the first place! When I ask my husband if my outfit looks good, I know it doesn't, and I really don't want him to answer the question I have just asked him! When I subconsciously pick a fight with my husband because my hormones or raging, I feel bloated, and he is a man! When my sock drawer looks like a tornado hit it, but I insist that the pillows on the couch are arranged just so.

What is your definition of crazy? Can you relate?

Re-create your strength

Middle School Rope Test

My first real athletic feat was in 6th grade. Awkward as most young girls are at that age. I was skinny and definitely not what I would consider athletic. I was fairly good at little league softball a but still did not consider myself an athlete.

Middle School PE class was the worst! Changing into shorts, t-shirts and gym shoes at the same time let you know each other's stage of puberty. Some were farther along than others, as was my case!

It was Rope Test day. From the gym ceiling, hung a rope that was 3 inches in diameter, and I have no idea how long. The test was to see how far you could climb up the rope. You did not have to climb all the way to the ceiling, there was a knot in the rope that was the high end point. The goal was to climb to the knot, touch the knot and then descend the rope.

I vividly remember watching several kids attempt the climb. A few made it, most did not. There was really no rhyme or reason either to who did and who did not. It was my turn. I was not too worried because while I did not think of myself as an athlete, I was a tomboy and spent many days climbing trees. I knew I could do it if I got a system down, and took my time. Sure enough! I put the rope between my feet and used my legs to push myself up the rope, then I would move my arms to pull a little further up. Repeat the process. It was a long process. I didn't sprint up that rope, yet I made it to the knot and was so proud of myself!

I never looked down, I kept moving upward, using what strength I had to conquer that rope. Some days we wake up want a do-over. Somedays we just was to sit at the bottom of the rope and feel sorry for ourselves. Don't. Get up, focus on Jesus and the strength you find in Him and move upward!

Don't miss out on your surroundings

One of my favorite things is to go for a long walk with my husband. I say "with" because we go together, at the same time, but he is always a few feet ahead of me! Walking for him is exercise, not something to be enjoyed. I saunter when I walk. I enjoy taking in the surroundings and talking while I walk. Jay just wants to hurry up and get it over with!

When we hurry along in life, we miss what is around us. Experience the journey.

On my bucket list was a trip to New York City at Christmas time. For my 50th birthday, my husband checked that off my list! I wanted to walk the streets of Manhattan and take in all the sights. Although I had been to NYC before but never at Christmas time.

We stood just outside Rockefeller Center and watched the light show on the side of Bloomingdales. We sat on the stands in Time Square and watched the world go by, literally. Time Square represented so many people from so many parts of our world! We walked a few blocks to Macy's and took time to study each of the windows gloriously decorated for Christmas. We just walked and walked and walked. We took in the Broadway production of " Wicked" which was absolutely fabulous! We ate a slice of pizza from a tiny pizza place. We talked to street vendors and purchased a Gyro from one.

It was magical! I saw everything I had dreamed to see! We took our time, slowed down our pace, took it all in!

Hurrying and rushing zaps your energy and doesn't allow you to take in life that is happening around you today! Slow down in this life, take it all in and re-create your strength.

Recreate your spirit

Are you talking to me?

When we moved our office into our home, it was just Jay and I. Soon we added an office person. Later we added a computer and design person. Both female. In our little 15 x 15 office, were 3 females, and one male, all working together.

Now I don't know if you have this "gift", but I can work on my computer and talk to myself all at the same time. Come to find out so did our office person and computer person! Jay however does not possess this gift.

One day, we were all hard at work, and I remember Jay pounded on his desk very loudly and asked in a very stern and direct voice, " Is anyone in here talking to me? Because if you are not, then please be quiet!" Apparently, the three of us women had all been working so diligently that we had not noticed that we were all talking to ourselves out loud!

This is how I pray as well. Sometimes I write my prayers, or sometimes I pray silently, but the best way for me to pray is talk to God out loud.

When I run, I pray. When I am driving, I pray. When I golf, I pray. When I shop, I pray. Prayer is simply conversing with God. I find if I talk out loud, it feels more like a conversation to me. Did you ever think about that verse - pray without ceasing?

This is how I pray continuously. The only way we can re-create our spirit is to converse with the One who created us.

Sexy Shoes

" If you repeat a lie often enough, people will begin to believe it is true"~ Adolf Hitler.

The lie we have bought into is that men and women are equal . I believe the woman's movement started because culture at that time proported the superiority of men. To overcome this belief system, women went the opposite direction and began to proport equality.

I am reminded of the words to the song from the musical, *Annie Get Your Gun,* "anything you can do, I can do better, I can do anything better than you" sung by the character, Annie.

The reality is this, we have both been created by God in His image YET fully male and fully female. Equal yet very different! It isn't about who can do what better but rather how God has created us male and female. This chapter is about embracing our sexuality as females created in the image of God fully feminine.

" So God created mankind in his own image, in the image of God he created them; male and female he created them." Genesis 1:27, NIV

God created woman last, the crown jewel of his creation! Women today feel as if we have to prove something, go it alone. Be strong and independent and if we aren't then we are letting down women everywhere!

I am Woman!

When I was growing up, one of my favorite female singers was Helen Reddy. A song she sung that was definitely a product of the women's rights movement was simply entitled. " I am Woman". I would sing that song at the top of my lungs, everywhere I went. Not because I was a proponent of the movement but rather because I was a young teenage girl grasping with the reality of who my God had created me to be.

A portion of the chorus goes like this, " I am strong, I am

invincible, I am woman". In these three phrases we find the keys to embracing our sexuality. Before we can move on, let's define these three words so we are all on the same page!

" I am strong"

I am not speaking of great physical strength. I am referring to women being able and capable. Our God created us with unique feminine strengths. Woman's intuition for example. Women just innately know in certain situations that something is off or evil that needs to be challenged or avoided. Multi-tasking is another strength of women. A woman's brain was created to be able to multi-task. Women can move between both sides of their brain simultaneouly.

" I am invincible"

The word invincible is defined as "incapable of being conquered, defeated or subdued. " In Jesus Christ we are invincible, not in our own power but through His.

" In all these things we are more than conquerors through Him who loved us" Romans 8:37

We have all been created as more than conquerors, men and women alike. This quality shows up in men as a"shoot 'em up, cowboy, ride in and save the day" mentality. In women it shows up as strong in heart.

"I am woman"

We are created female, in the image and likeness of God. In our culture of gender equality and gender definition, we have done ourselves a disservice in not embracing our femininity. I am not speaking to whether you are a "girly girl" or a "tomboy". I am referring Genesis 1:27 "So God created man in his own image, in the image of God created he him; **male and female** created he **them**." God created us female, in His image and in His likeness, embrace all He has created you to be!

46

Those who have gone before us

Let's look at strong invincible women in the Bible.

Noah's wife- Gn 6:18, 7:7

We never know her name. In the story of Noah in the Bible, it is all about Noah. In fact if you read the account, often is it worded, " Noah, his sons, his wife, and his son's wives"' Let's look at this no-name woman.

She married a righteous man. Noah was the only righteous man God could find to save the world. So we can assume she was wise and smart because she picked Noah! The Bible describes Noah as righteous, blameless and walked with God. (Gen 6:9) Therefore we can also assume that she was righteous as well. God did choose to save and her three sons in the Ark.

She was a faithful helper, for crying out loud her husband was the laughingstock of the world for over 100 years yet she stood by him as he built his ark and was a zookeeper! She did not laugh at him or what he heard God tell him do. Instead she worked alongside of him. Noah's wife was strong. She raised her children in a world she knew would be destroyed. She was invincible. She was a woman. She knew what Noah needed to accomplish what God had called him to do. She stood by him. She knew they were going to be on an ark for 40 days and nights as the floods would come. She was not to be defeated.

Esther-Esther 2:15

She found favor with all who knew her. She was naturally a well liked person, a gift given to her by God. The job He had for her to do, she needed to be well-like in order to accomplish it.

She had charm and grace that attracted people to her. This was her feminity at it's core. I imagine her being a woman that when she walked through town everyone stopped and looked at her. Not only because she was physically beautiful, but because there was an air about her that

> *She had charm and grace that attracted people to her. This was her feminity at it's core.*

47

exuded charisma.

Esther was willing to give her life to save her people. Going to the king uninvited as she did was very dangerous. She knew what she had to do to expose Haman's plot and save her people even though it may cost her life. Esther was a conqueror, invincible,unstoppable because she knew her God had given her a job to do and she was going to do it regardless of the cost.

Eunice- Acts 16:1 2 Timothy 3:15

Her name means trainer, happily conquering. It is believed that Eunice was Timothy's mother who raised her son in the knowledge of the scripture. He went on to be one of the favored men of the New Testament. A founder of our faith. I find it ironic that she is mentioned in the bible concerning child rearing and her name means happily conquering!

She was gifted by God to train up her children. Her strength was found in understanding this was her calling in life. Even her name identifies who she was.

Happily conquering, but conquering! She was invincible!

A mother, a wife, a Godly woman fulfilling her life's mission.

Abigail – 1 Samuel 25;3, 14:42 (24)

Leader of the dance; joy

She was a beautiful woman, intelligent and diplomatic! Her husband Nabal had no idea that David and his men were protecting his shepherds. When they asked for food, Nabal refused and ranted at David. David vowed to kill Nabal's men. Abigail steps in and heads David off. Protecting both her husband and his men but she protected David as well.

"May you be blessed for your good judgment and for keeping me from bloodshed this day and from avenging myself with my own hands."
1 Sam. 25:33

She was strong.

48

She was invincible. Meeting with an angry David and his angry men was brave. She offered peace and food. David accepted. In doing this she also went against her husband, knowing that she would endure his anger as well. Abigail was the woman God made her to be, eventually becoming David's wife, she used her femininity as God created her to disarm and smooth out an otherwise volatile situation.

Rahab – Joshua 2:1-22, 6:17, 22-25, Heb 11:1

A prostitute used by God for His purposes! She had to be strong! She defied her king and her country and helped servants of God.

Her faith made her invincible. She had faith that if she helped the men of God escape over the wall, though she might die yet she knew that God would take care of her. She faced reality and understood who she was- a woman rejected by society, and outcast and yet God still used her to bring his bloodline into the world.

God created us male and female, both in His image for His glory. As women, at times, we have cheapened our femininity and tried to become more male rather than embracing who God made us, fully female - strong, invincible, and woman.

Hurried Woman Syndrome

Several years ago, I came across study online conducted by Dr. Brent Bost which he has now published a book, entitled, "The Hurried Woman Syndrome". Basically the facts are this: 30 million women suffer from this syndrome. Affecting women between the ages of 25 and 55 who have children between the ages of 4 and 16.

"What causes the Hurried Woman Syndrome?
"Actually, stress is probably the single most important factor that causes women to complain about the Hurried Woman Syndrome. There are many types of stress and they vary from patient to patient. Sometimes the stress can't be avoided, such as a sick child or a high-powered career. However, for the majority of women, much of the stress is avoidable or at least could be

managed better. These avoidable stresses are those that often come from a busy, hectic schedule and lifestyle choices that many of us have embraced as completely "normal." Yet, the effects of this kind of stress --- what I call "hurry" --- can have very significant long-term and wide-reaching consequences for the woman who labors under it and those around her who suffer along with her." Dr. Brent Bost, http://www.hurriedwoman.com/syndrome.html

Dr. Bost goes onto discuss about the physical symptoms that appear when a woman is suffering from this syndrome. Do any of these sound familiar? Fatigue, low sex drive, and weight gain. Could it be that we are trying so hard to prove ourselves, our worth, our equality, that we are making ourselves sick?

I want to encourage us as women to embrace all God has created in us. We are created in His image, in His likeness, fully female. He has gifted us in ways that He intends to use for His kingdom and we try to be something that we are not, His kingdom loses.

Slippers

Typical Day

My day starts at 6 am. My alarm blares in my ear, startling me awake rather than the slow natural awakening I would prefer! I stumble out of bed, into the bathroom, rub my sleepy eyes and my day begins.

My goal is to get downstairs and have at least one cup of coffee before anyone else comes downstairs. Jay is not too far behind, stumbling downstairs and searching longingly for his cup of coffee!

After a cup of coffee has done the trick and awoken me, I can then pack lunches and fix breakfasts. While Grace, our daughter, is preparing for school, I am reading, studying and enjoying another cup of coffee.

Helping, shoving,and or encouraging Grace out the door at 7:40, results in my turn to get ready to attack the day. This involves basic primping and deciding what to wear for the day. Which is a lengthy decision!

By lunchtime, I have completed any household chores, made my task list for work, checked and answered email, and run 4 miles. The afternoon is for meetings, writing, and appointments with staff.

3 pm comes, and it is time to greet Grace coming home from school, converse about her day, assign her household chores, and or homework, then back to wrap up whatever work is still yet to be done.

Around the 6 o'clock hour tummies are ready for dinner! After dinner is cooked, eaten and cleaned up and it is slipper time! My day is done except for the relaxing part and relaxing is best accomplished in slippers!

Slipper Time!

The person that we are when we put on our slippers is who we are at our core, when no one is looking. You put your slippers on when you walk in the door from a long day when your feet are tired and you are ready to relax. You throw off the cares and stress of the day and come home to the person you really are.

Your day may not look anything like mine, but at some point in your "coming home" you will throw off the day and slip into your slippers!
What do your slippers look like? Are they some fluffy animal or some wild animal print? Are they stiff clogs, practical slip on or are they cozy? Slippers tell us a lot about who we are.

Slipper Purchases

This year, my shoe purchase over Spring Break, was a new pair of fuzzy, animal print slippers. I love them! My family, not so much! Jay said I could get them as long as I only wore them in the house and not in public as I have been known to walk out of the house, accidentally, with my slippers on.

Grace, my daughter, declared that my new fuzzy animal print slippers, " are so you mom!" And they are! You might not choose animal print or fuzzy slippers. You might choose some-thing more conservative and practical but still comfortable. Our slippers reflect who we are at home, when no one else is around.

Authentic and Transparent

We need to mesh the person we are in pub-lic with the person we are when no one else is around. That is authenticity. How can we become authentic and transparent women in a culture where most wom-en are working tirelessly to be someone that they are not? We need to be authentic. Our husbands, our children, our families, our friends, co-workers, our world needs authentic women.

> *We need to be authentic. Our husbands, our children, our families, our friends, co-workers, our world needs authentic women.*

52

We need to be transparent women in a world where no one wants anyone else to see their "baggage" We need to learn to live a life where others can see who we are inside of us and we allow them to without fear of being judged or rejected.

We live in a world where we spend countless hours on Facebook, looking into someone else's life, wondering why we can't have and do and be who and what they are.

Comfortable in our own skin

When our daughter, Grace, was a preschooler, she attended a small private Christian preschool. The class size was maybe 6 children. Her teacher was a wonderful woman, Mrs. Eich, who handled preschool children better than anyone I had ever met!

Grace has always had her own way of living life! She, even now at 16, is her own person and lives life as she sees fit, even if it isn't the "norm". As a preschooler, this was evidenced in the clothing she wore! She didn't like the cute little outfits I bought. She had to take a top of one outfit and put it with bottoms to another. Stripes with polka dots, plaids with stripes, purple with orange, red with hot pink.

Through wearing some of the craziest ensembles, she explored her love of color and fashion at a very young age and to this day puts outfits together and colors together I would never put together, but that is who she is. A phrase we say often about Grace is that she is "comfortable in her own skin" and that defines her to a tee.

In order to be authentic and transparent women we have to be comfortable in our own skin. Comfortable with whom we have been created to be. We are our own person, we are uniquely created so there is only one of us. We have heard it 1000 times if we have heard it once but we need to let it sink in- real beauty is on the inside not only the outside. It is more than skin deep.

In order to become authentic and transparent women, we must become "comfortable in our own skin".

COMFORTABLE: Contented and undisturbed

Every Sunday, after church and after lunch, it is nap- time in the Laffoon house! I change out of church clothes, (including the bra!) put on a sweatshirt, and my comfy sweats! Jay hates them! You could say my comfy sweats are less than attractive...they are gray and baggy and oh so comfy! My children know that if the comfy sweats go on then stay away- it is napping time!

Maybe you have comfy sweats. Maybe you have a comfortable chair. Or maybe you have comfortable Pajamas. Whatever it is, we all understand that feeling of being comfortable.

Coming to grips with this word "comfortable" as it pertains to be authentic and transparent means we have to capture that feeling we feel when we put on our comfy sweats or sink down into our comfy chair. "AHHHH I am home" feeling!

FB speaks

I decided to pose the question to ladies on FB. " Are you comfortable with who you are? What areas do you feel good about and in what areas do you struggle?"

The overwhelming response on FB to the question " Are you comfortable with who you are?", was no. A few women responded yes, but shared the struggle and long process of getting there! The reasons for women not being comfortable with who they are varied but the majority pointed to weight or their body image in general.

What was interesting in the responses I received was that the majority were uncomfortable with who they are yet the reasons they sited varied greatly.

Here are a few of those responses:

"All my life I've made decisions based on what I thought would please others - parents (even a mother who passed away 24 years ago), husband, kids, teachers, friends, pastors, etc. I had listened to the critical voices that had said I was too heavy and other stuff. When I realized I had lived longer than my mother,

54

I decided it was time to make my decisions based on who God created me to be. It's not a sudden change, but a gradual transformation. And I think it is allowing some healing to happen in my marriage."

"I had been bullied a lot in life. People telling me I was ugly. Even family. Never feeling like I belonged. I had gotten to the point where I believe what people said. I tried to hard to get people to like me, and it just caused people to turn away. I am so self conscious now! I can't stand to look in the mirror at times. It is a big struggle!"

"I don't feel like I know my calling or purpose. I decided it was really important for me and my children to be a stay at home mom. My oldest is 21 now and youngest is 7. So I struggle with doubts, should I have finished college and had a career. It feels like no one values what I do as a mom and wife. I have gained about 45 lbs over the years, been up and down. I don't like what I see in the mirror or worse pictures. I won't even buy a bathing suit. My husband had a 6 month affair, I just learned about recently. We are trying to stay together, but it is very difficult to believe any kind words from him at this point. I can pray and have faith for other people's situations and God really moves, but not so much my own."

I am sure we find a bit of ourselves in each of these answers. Being authentic and transparent is being comfortable with who we are, inside and out. As you can see in the responses from ladies who answered my question, that is very hard to live out. Our culture focuses so much on the outer beauty that becoming comfortable in our skin is a daily, minute by minute struggle, and the struggle is real.

We are bombarded with this new diet pill that will make us as skinny as the celebrity spokesperson hawking it on television. An ad pops up on our Facebook page that prods us to get the latest and greatest wrinkle cream. When we do, we find ourselves looking in the mirror convincing ourselves it is working(not that I have ever done that)! How can we become comfortable, content and undisturbed, with who we are in a world that is constantly harassing us to change our appearance?

I believe the answer is found in Colossians 3:10.

"and have put on the new self who is being [a]renewed to a true knowledge according to the image of the One who created him"

Everyday, as you wake up, you put on a new self! One that has the knowledge that you have been created by a loving creative God! He made you the way He did for his purpose! I want you to visually, everyday, get up and as you get dressed for your day I want you to put on a new self as well! Focus on the One who created you you. You have been made in His image (Genesis 1:27). Stop and let that sink in. You have been fearfully and wonderfully made (Psalms 139:14.) Write on that mirror that you look into everyday scripture that will remind you of these facts!

Being comfortable with you are will allow you to live the life God created you to live and accomplish what He needs you to for His kingdom.

OWN: of or pertaining to oneself

Jay and I were cutting up veggies together, talking about life. I made a comment about someone, he replied, " You are mean!" I retorted, " Yes I am and I own it." It is who I am, good or bad. I have the spiritual gift of sarcasm. At times, those sarcastic words may sound mean and at times it is how I make a living (being funny that is)!

Owning who we are, being our own person is understanding God made you uniquely you and me uniquely me, quirks and all. There is not another Laura Laffoon on the planet! My family might be a bit excited about that, but it is the truth! There is not another you either.

- Your shape
- Your size
- Your abilities
- Your journey
- Your story, all you and not anyone else.

A God who loves us more than we can ever think or imagine has created each of us as an individual. He only created one of you!

Now own it! Quit trying to change who you were created to be! Yes, there can be improvements; we all need to grow as individuals, but too many of us waste too much time and energy trying to recreate what the Creator already created!

How do we own who we are, especially if we may not like who we are? 1 Peter 3:4, "but *let it be* the hidden person of the heart, with the imperishable quality of a gentle and quiet spirit, which is precious in the sight of God." NASB. The hidden person of the heart is who we are when no one else is around, our core, our heart. Own the hidden person of the heart.

In all honesty, I struggled with this verse all my life!. There is nothing gentle and quiet about Laura Laffoon! Often when I would read this verse I focused on that part of the verse. There were times in my life I tried to be gentle and quiet and it just didn't feel right. I never felt as if I was being who God created me to be.

One day as I was lamenting before the Lord that I was never going to be gentle and quiet, it came to me that this is talking about being gentle and quiet before the Lord. Taking time to be quiet in His presence and let Him speak to me. I think of gentle as being calm and peaceful. Gentle before the Lord , remaining calm and enjoy peace in Him. Whew! I can do that!

Owning who we are, accepting our quirks, our abilities, our journey, our hidden person of the heart, is only done by being gentle and quiet in God's presence. When we take time to be with him and allow him to speak to us, we will begin to understand and own who he has made us to be.
As you stand in front of that mirror every morning, put on that new self and thank the Lord for the way He has put you together. Thank Him for the way He has wired you.

Owning you, realizing there is only one you and that is on purpose will allow you to live the life God created you to live and accomplish what He needs you to for His kingdom.

SKIN: Outer layer; to strip off

When my daddy would be getting ready to discipline me as a child he would always use a very southern phrase. He would say, " I am going to skin your hide". I always found it very amusing. It didn't make sense to me as a child, and still doesn't as an adult! What he was really saying was that was a spanking in my future! I am pretty sure there were better ways to communicate that fact!

However, as we think of becoming authentic and transparent women, we do have to "skin our hides". Hebrews 12:1 encourages us to throw off anything that hinders us and any sin that might entangle us and run with perseverance the race that has been laid out before us.

As we will discuss in a future chapter, Hiking boots, we have all been given a unique life journey. No ones life is exactly like another. We have to journey down our path, not someone else's. In order to do this with authenticity and transparency, we must throw off all that holds us back.

Have you ever attended a masquerade party? The purpose of a masquerade party is for everyone to come to the party dressed with a mask covering their face up. At an appointed time everyone removes their mask to reveal who they really are. That is a good picture of what I am talking about here in being authentic and transparent.

We all wear masks to hide who we really are. If we truly want to be authentic and transparent we have to remove those masks.

"The irony of the masks is that although we wear them to make other people think well of us, they are drawn to us only when we take them off." JOHN ORTBERG

Read that again! That is a powerful statement! We try to cover who we are so others will think more highly of us or will like us better but in reality when we let them see who we really are,baggage and all, that is the person others will truly appreciate.

We put on two masks – one of perfection because we want

people to think we have it all together! We want to seem as if we have the perfect home, job, spouse, children, etc. We put on the mask of pretense; we pretend to be something or someone that we are not.

Mask of Perfection

None of us is perfect so why do we hide behind this mask?

When Jay and I married I was not the best housekeeper! I actually despised cleaning. Toilets are disgusting to clean and even more so if you don't clean them regularly! Vacuuming could be done every day twice a day and the floors would still look unkept. It all seemed like a waste of time to me!

So here was my plan. I figured if I made everything look clean on the first floor of the house, no one would really know that my closets were a disaster, that the second floor of the house was really dusty, or that my laundry was piled up and hidden behind a closed door! We may have looked good on the outside but on the inside we were a disaster! Guests would come over and always comment how nice and clean our house was! My reply was always, " if you only knew"!

Many of us live our lives this way. We look really good on the outside but the inside is a disaster. Further, we would be horrified to let anyone know! Being authentic means we have to be real and not fake. We have to let others see that we are a disaster at times, and life isn't always what it seems on the outside!

Mask of Pretense

Playing pretend, as a child was fun and imaginative. Playing pretend, as an adult is hurtful and deceiving.

Have you ever had a conversation with a friend, who shared with you something in confidence, and you turn around and find yourself telling someone else? Or someone messed up or failed in some way and you gossiped about it?

Pretending you care when you really don't? You may say but I don't do that! Oh really have you ever asked someone in passing, " how are you doing?" and then didn't even listen to their answer? Or the reverse, someone asks you how you are doing and you say you are doing fine, when in reality, you are about to fall apart?

Facebook has brought on a whole new level of pretending. We can "put our best face forward" so to speak. When we rip off that skin and let those around us see beyond the mask of perfection and pretense, we become vulnerable in a whole new way. This fact is why so many of us prefer to stay behind the mask!

2 Corinthians 3:18 "But we all, with unveiled face, beholding as in a mirror the glory of the Lord, are being transformed into the same image from glory to glory, just as from the Lord, the Spirit."

The only way we can truly rip off the skin and reveal our authentic and transparent self is to look in a mirror.

On any given day how much time do you spend on yourself, looking in mirror, shower, makeup clothing, as opposed to how much time do you spend with Jesus? Ladies there is the rub. If when we look in a mirror we would see ourselves as Jesus see us, we would have no need for masks. We would become comfortable in our own skin!

This task isn't easy and not without pain! When I was young, and actually still to this day, I couldn't for the life of me rip a bandaid off my body! The unknown pain frightened me. Ripping of the masks we hide behind and becoming comfortable in our own skin is just like ripping off a bandaid. We are frightened of what might be behind the mask. We are frozen with fear to let others see us as we are. We are paralyzed with the pain imagined in our minds, that may or may not be real! We must get a grip on that mask, just like a bandaid, and rip it off, knowing that we have been made by a God who loves us and created us for His purpose!

Coming to Grips

Coming to grips with being "comfortable in our own skin" is like sinking into that favorite chair or slipping into those favorite slippers- it is accepting the woman God has created you to be. Own that woman. Be all she was created to be and not someone
60

else. Throw off those masks that cover the real you!

Transparent defined is not blocked, letting the light shine through. The only way to be comfortable in your own skin is to do just that. Don't block the woman God created you to be. Let the light shine through you, the real you needs to be let out. God only created one of you and if you continue to try to be someone you are not, the real you never lives and never accomplishes what you were created to do and be for the Kingdom!

Dancing Shoes

It was a beautiful Fall Sunday. Our church was hosting a ministry festival right after worship to acquaint people with various ministries and life groups.

Pizza, soft drinks, a live band, face painting, bouncey houses and children running every where were all apart of the scene that was before me at the Married Life Ministry booth.

My eyes were drawn to a little girl; she couldn't have been more than 10, in the corner of the lawn all by herself. She was moving to the music with her hands in the air, like a dancer, swaying, leaping, and moving in her own world. Totally unaware of the hundreds of people milling around the lawn. She was dancing!

As I watched her, I was struck by the fact that she was so absorbed in her dance she didn't even see anyone else. She was dancing with clear abandon!

We can experience life with abandon just like the little girl who danced. We just have to strap on our dancing shoes and dance, dance, dance!

Abandon and Control

I want to live with abandon but what exactly does that mean or look like? Abandon means to give up control; to yield oneself without restraint and or moderation. Control is to have power over something; to exercise direction over.

Whew! I need to give up control in order to live with abandon and by definition that means giving up power and direction over my life! In conclusion we can live with abandon by giving up control to Jesus. Which sounds much easier than it actually is!

In order to live with abandon we need to take three dance steps: relax, release and rest.

Aspiring Dancer

I took dance as a young girl but I regretfully quit at a young age. When our daughter Grace was 3, we enrolled her in a dance class. She loved it! When Grace began dance it stirred in me that desire to dance again. I really wanted to take a tap class. Finally when Grace was in 7th grade, it fit in my schedule to take an adult tap class at the same time she had a dance class! I loved it!

In my first recital, I played Elphaba, the green witch from *Wicked*. It was so much fun and nerve wracking at the same time. I knew the steps. I knew the dance. I was on stage every week-end with Jay speaking this should not be difficult! Yet it was! I remember sweating profusely backstage before it was our turn to perform. People ask me all the time if I get nervous before a show with Jay. I don't get nervous nor do I experience stage fright. But this day I did.

Finally when it was our turn, we took our places on the blacked out stage. In those few seconds of darkness, I remember giving myself a pep talk. I knew the steps. I knew the dance. I just needed to relax and let go and dance! We did well, and I had great fun!

Living with abandon is living in such a way that you just relax, let go and dance!

Dance step 1: Relax

It is an Art!

Relaxing has never been a difficult idea for me to grasp! It might be one of my spiritual gifts.

A few years ago we converted a bonus room over our garage into a two -room office suite. We worked in one room and the other room housed media for the kids. Once the kids were grown , I moved out of the shared office a few months ago and created my own office space! It was wonderful for me...Jay on the other-hand had difficulty adjusting. But I digress....

When we moved into our home offices, Jay had a hard

time shutting it down at night. I would find him in the office, after hours, reading email, writing a letter, or checking something else off his task list. It got so bad that we finally had a heart to heart discussion. The deal became that after office hours, I was going to shut the door to the office and he was not to open it again until 8 am the next morning.

What we learned from this habit of shutting the office door was that Jay needed something to occupy his mind and time so he could relax at night, as well as a relaxing place. We created some relaxing areas in our house. We turned half of the office into a library which contains comfortable chairs and a couch for reading. We equipped a back porch space that is comfortable and relaxing for the few summer months here in Michigan. Lastly we designed a front porch space for those in-between months in Fall and Spring. None of this took a lot of money, mostly just moving furniture from other parts of the house!

After creating the space, we developed a routine. Office hours are completed with the onset of dinner, regardless of the season. In the winter months, after dinner, we go to the library for reading or "fun" computer work on an iPad. Fun being researching our next vacation, or some friendly app games to keep our minds sharp! Actually, we aren't legalistic about what we do it just can't be work! In the summer, after dinner, we can be found on the back porch. This has been a great habit we have developed in order to relax, and it has spilled over into the lives of our kids, who relax with us!

Relaxing our minds as well as our bodies allows us to recuperate and re-energize. I don't know about you but at the end of most days, my brain is tired. I often tell Jay, " My brain stops working at 6 p.m." It just does. I cannot absorb any more information or string any more words together in a sentence. The creative juices are all gone! I need to recuperate from my day.

> *Relaxing our minds as well as our bodies allows us to recuperate and re-energize.*

When I take the time to relax, I am also re-energized for the next day. My brain has taken time off of work related information and moved on to something mundane, whether I read a book or play Words with Friends. I need the time for my brain to focus elsewhere!

This is Hard Work!

Relaxing in this techno world is hard to do. Our daughter Grace goes to bed with an iPad for watching movies or listening to music, and an iPhone for her alarm. When she was younger, she always went to bed listening to Adventures in Odyssey. It soothed her to listen to the story and helped her fall asleep. The amazing part was she learned Bible stories and lessons while she was dozing off to sleep!

Now that she's older, relaxing for Grace comes in a different form than it does for me. After a day at school, and then swim team practice, she walks in the door of the house and needs some Grace time. We feed her and then she goes to her room to relax; away from people and away from conversation. After an hour or so, she is good. She can do homework, or have conversation with Mom and Dad. She has recuperated from her day and is now re-energized.

One of my favorite books that I have discovered in the last few years, are the Jesus Calling books by Sarah Young.

"Relax and let me lead you through this day. I have everything under control: My control. You tend to peer anxiously into the day that is before you, trying to figure out what to do, and when. Meanwhile, the phone or the doorbell rings, and you have to reshuffle your plans. All that planning ties you up in knots and distracts you from Me. Attentiveness to Me is not only for your quiet time, but for all your time. As you look to Me, I show you what to do now and next. Vast quantities of time and energy are wasted in obsessive planning. When you let Me direct your steps, you are set free to enjoy Me and to find what I have prepared for you this day."

Young, Sarah (2004-10-12). Jesus Calling (p. 218). Thomas Nelson. Kindle Edition.

Relaxing is the first step in living with abandon. We have to allow our brains and bodies to relax in order to give up control and allow the Spirit to take over.

66

Dance Step 2: Release

Living in the moment

I truly believe that your best quality can also be your worst at times. One quality that I have that exemplifies this is living in the moment, or spontaneity. Growing up I was not much of a planner, or a goal setter and lived on a whim. In the the words of *Scarlett O'Hara, Gone with the Wind*, "I will worry about that tomorrow"!!

Jay is very much a planner, and goal setter. We butted heads a lot when we were first married because I was more "live and let live" and he was all about the plan. Our kids to this day will ask, " so what is the plan for today".

Over the years, I have developed a mentality of goal setting and planning; to the point of pushing aside that spontaneous quality.

Recently, I had a friend who experienced a death in her family. As I was reading and praying in the morning, I distinctly felt the Lord prompting me to text her and offer to bring food for incoming family that would be gathering at her house. I felt the prompting and then began to think of all the excuses I could not to do it. Wouldn't it be presumptuous of me to assume she needed food? Wouldn't she be offended that I would only be able to bring store bought stuff? I don't have time to do this. I am way too busy! I don't want to intrude at this time of loss. The list went on and on.

After a few minutes of arguing with myself and the Lord, making excuses that were just that, excuses. I decided to be spontaneous and do it. I texted my friend and told her I was bringing food and then promptly went to the grocery store and picked up a bunch of items to take to her home that afternoon. She was very grateful.

Sometimes we get so caught up in our plan for the day that we don't leave any room for the prompting of the Holy Spirit in us to live in the moment. Having a plan for

> *Sometimes we get so caught up in our plan for the day that we don't leave any room for the prompting of the Holy Spirit in us to live in the moment.*

your day, week, or month is a good idea and necessary for some. However living with abandon involves living in the moment from time to time.

Letting go of the steering wheel

I have never in my life thought of myself as a control freak! I think that whole live in the moment quality overrode any thought of being in control. I always saw myself as more laissez-faire. Life has a funny way of pointing out qualities you never thought you had!

When our daughter Grace started learning to drive, I became very adept at coming up with reasons for Jay to drive with her! Use this as a good bonding time! You are the better driver! You taught Torrey to drive! I have a headache! I became very good at it, so good, that I don't think I drove in the car with her alone, without Jay, the entire time she was getting her learner's permit!

Then she turned 16. Now the inevitable was going to happen. At some point I was going to ride in the car with her alone. I don't remember the time or place but I do remember keeping my hand firmly planted on the emergency break the entire time so when we got home my entire arm hurt from gripping too tightly! Subsequently every time after that whenever I had to ride with her I firmly planted my hand on the emergency brake.

Grace is a very good driver! I came to that realization very quickly but I could not for some reason let go of that emergency brake! I have come to understand that in letting go of that brake I would be letting go of complete control. Not only of the car but of Grace. She is growing up and will soon be moving on to college. It was more than her driving, it was her life.

This is where the Rubber meets the Road

After we have relaxed our mind and bodies, the next step is to release. This is the hard reality of turning the controls over to the Holy Spirit and allowing Him to give us the ability to hear his voice. If we haven't allowed our brains and bodies to recuperate and re-energize, we won't be in a place to hear Him. Our bodies will be too tired to respond to what He is calling us to do at that moment. Our brains will be too filled with our "to do list" know that
68

it is His voice speaking to us.

"Whenever you start to feel anxious, remind yourself that your security rests in Me alone, and I am totally trustworthy. You will never be in control of your life circumstances, but you can relax and trust in My control. Instead of striving for a predictable, safe lifestyle, seek to know Me in greater depth and breadth. I long to make your life a glorious adventure, but you must stop clinging to old ways. I am always doing something new within My beloved ones. Be on the lookout for all that I have prepared for you."
Young, Sarah (2004-10-12). Jesus Calling (p. 197). Thomas Nelson. Kindle Edition.

Dance Step 3: Rest

I am a sleeper!

I love sleep! Do you? It is a fact! Sometimes I actually crave going to bed! Just to feel my head hit the pillow and my body sink into my soft mattress…ahhhh…. I do think sleep is a form of rest obviously; it is when our bodies rest. In Genesis 2:3 the Bible tells is the God rested after all the work He had done. WE need to rest our bodies. But the rest I am referring to here is brain rest, soul rest, and spiritual rest.

"Come to me, all you who are weary and burdened, and I will give you rest. Take my yoke upon you and learn from me, for I am gentle and humble in heart, and you will find rest for your souls. For my yoke is easy and my burden is light." Matthew 11:28-29

Many times when life gets stressful and I am feeling anxious, after Grace leaves for school, I will return to bed, not to sleep necessarily but to pray. I lay in bed, then starting with my toes, I relax and then I pray.

We may all find our minds resting in different places. Jay finds rest on the golf course. Sometimes I find rest while I am running. It is quiet, I am outdoors alone, and can think and pray. All too often we try and fix everything in our own strength. We strive, struggle vigorously, worry, incessantly and we think we can take care of ourselves and or everyone else. When we do this is zaps our energy, our joy, we become drained and cranky, grouchy...

When in actuality all we need to do is rest in Jesus. Take time to give Him your burdens, your worries, your cares, cry out to him; shed the tears, yell and scream!

In Jesus is where we find rest.

I couldn't say it any better.

> *In Jesus is where we find rest.*

"Rest with me a while. You have journeyed up a steep, rugged path in recent days. The way ahead is shrouded in uncertainty. Look neither behind you nor before you. Instead, focus your attention on Me, your constant Companion. Trust that I will equip you fully for whatever awaits you on your journey. I designed time to be a protection for you. You couldn't bear to see all your life at once. Though I am unlimited by time, it is in the present moment that I meet you. Refresh yourself in My company, breathing deep draughts of My Presence. The highest level of trust is to enjoy Me moment by moment. I am with you, watching over you wherever you go."

Young, Sarah (2004-10-12). Jesus Calling (p. 187). Thomas Nelson. Kindle Edition.

We are creatures of control. We want to control our own lives. We want to control those around us and make them do what we want them to do, whether it is our mate, children, or friends. We want to control the situation.

We live in an on demand world where we control what we watch on TV and when. We can listen to music or podcasts, sermons, 24/7. We can text people we don't want to talk to over the phone, whenever and wherever we want.

We think we are in control however we can't live with abandon before the Lord and maintain control of our lives

Similar to a flag on a flagpole waving in the wind - the wind controls the flag. When it is whipping and whirling so is the flag. When it is still the flag does not move.

70

In Psalms 46:10, we are told to "Be still and know" that He is God. We have to first relax, quiet our minds and bodies. Once we can release control and realize that God is in control. Then, we can rest in Him, and allow Him bring the glory through our life that is due Him.

Putting on your dancing shoes and living life with abandon means relaxing so we can hear God prompt us to live in the moment, release and let Him be in control and rest in the fact that He has our journey mapped out.

Snow Shoes

Ecclesiastes 3:1 "For everything there is a season, a time for every purpose under heaven." (KJV)

I have 9 more sleeps left!

Sleep is my method for counting the days until Jay and I take our daughter to college. We will be dropping off our 17 year old baby in the middle of NYC! She is excited to follow her dream! Me? Not so much! I am actually kidding. I am very excited for her! She will be attending The King's College in Manhattan, pursuing a degree in Media, Culture, and the Arts, to hopefully one day become a writer.

It is the end of a chapter of our lives, and the beginning of a new one. For 25 years, we have been a family of four under one roof. Now we are a family of 5 (and a grand dog!), stretched from Michigan to New York.

As we all venture through seasons in our lives we realize that they come and go and we can make it through each one with dignity, grace and determination. Sometimes they last for 25 years and others for much less. At times getting through a season might seem like a never ending chore. Others may be over before you even know you were there.

My Favorite Season

We all understand the word season. If I had to state my favorite season it would be fall! I love the leaves changing color and the brisk coolness of the air. Fall takes us into the holiday season which is another reason why it is my favorite!

The time between Thanksgiving and Christmas is special as we have much to celebrate in our family. We have Thanksgiving, 3 birthdays, our wedding anniversary, and then Christmas. Early in our marriage, Jay and I established that this season would be one big party in our family!

The season starts with Thanksgiving dinner being scheduled around The Macy's Thanksgiving Day parade and Detroit Lions football. We eat a lot on Thanksgiving day. We have brunch as a family(our kids and Jay's parents, sister, and aunt) usually to include sausage, biscuits, gravy, and cheese grits before the football game.

After football, it is dinner time! After our bellies are full, we each take turns reflecting on the past year and the events or people we are thankful for and share them as a family. The day is then done and we all sleep like babies with full bellies!

The day after Thanksgiving, is our family's designated decorating day! The tree goes up amidst Christmas music blaring. Decorations are hung and displayed inside and out.

Birthday celebrations then ensue on Thanksgiving weekend. We celebrate Diane's, my sister-n-law, our son, Torrey, and mine. One big party with food and presents of course.

Jay and I usually celebrate our anniversary by getting away for a few days alone which is a nice break during this crazy season!

The celebration begins by attending Christmas Eve services followed by a family dinner. Then the morning comes! After the chaos of wrapping paper being strewn everywhere and squeals of delight over the perfect gift, we gather for brunch.

The season draws to a close as we turn out the lights of the tree at the end of a blessed day.

This season of the year can be chaotic and joy-filled all at the same time. Yet it is my favorite season! The chaos of the busyness of this season coupled with the joy being together causes my heart to stir.

Yes there are times during this season that we bicker at each other and become selfish for our own time. We become tired and ornery. I keep my eye on all the many reasons our family celebrates during this time, and all that seems to fade in the back-
74

ground.

Season: A Play on Words

When we hear the word, season, we naturally think about the four seasons-winter, spring, summer, and fall. Season is a period of time. It can be the cyclical year of weather change. It can be a season of illness. It can be a stage of life- high school, college, diapers, menopause.

Season can also be defined as "to mature, ripen, add character to". As we go through these periods of time, seasons, with dignity, grace, and determination,through these experiences, we become seasoned. Walking through a season with dignity involves plowing through with self-respect, not a whiny, poor me attitude. Grace walks through a season granting mercy. Enduring a season with determination requires you have a firm sight on a greater purpose.

Snowshoe: A contrivance (device) that may be attached to the foot to enable the wearer to walk on the deep snow without sinking. (dictionary.com)

As we strap on snowshoes of dignity, grace and determination we can plow through whatever season we find ourselves in without sinking!

Dignity

Jay's mom has spoiled my kids from the moment she heard we were pregnant! Clothes, shoes, toys, food, you name it they got whatever they wanted from Grandma- sometimes to her detriment!

Grandma purchased Torrey a shirt when he was 2, that didn't fit and needed to be returned. It was a snowy icy day when she returned the shirt to the mall. As she was returning to the car she slipped on black ice in the mall parking lot and shatter her lower leg in 14 places.

The doctors put her a contraption that encircled her leg piercing her skin in 14 locations. 14 pins held the bones in place to allow them to heal. Mom and Dad were told it would be 6-9 weeks that she would be in this device. It was a season. It was a season that lasted not 6-9 weeks, but 9 months!

A season of Dad doing all the housework, the laundry, the cooking, and taking care of Mom. Everyday, twice a day, Dad had to clean around pin spots where the pin entered into Mom's leg. He got down on his hands and knees twice a day and inflicted excruciating pain on his bride.

Mom's entire world was turned upside down as she was not one to sit around and do nothing! Yet here she was bed-ridden. Her bed was moved down to an area off the kitchen. She said it was easier for Dad, but I think she didn't want to miss anything!

She worked from her bed, she shopped from her bed, she played with Torrey from her bed.

It was a season. A painful season. A long season. Yet I cannot ever remember either of them complaining, whining, having a poor me attitude. Mom and Dad plowed through this season with dignity.

This season of illness definitely added character to each of them and matured their marriage as walking through it drew them closer together.

Grace

Walking through a season with Grace might just be the hardest to accomplish. It involves granting mercy and forgiveness.

Due to my line of work - marriage education - the season that comes to mind is one of marital conflict. Conflict is a given in any marriage. If you are married, you and your spouse experience conflict. If you don't then one of you must be dead!

Too many times in marriage, the conflict remains unresolved. A conflict arises, hurtful words are spoken, each walk away, the hurt buries deeper, no constructive words are spoken, no I'm sorry, no forgiveness and it cycles downward. Then the next conflict arises, and it begins all over, until the marriage has become a season of conflict and hurt and devaluing each other.

My mother-in- law is a very wise woman. She said this,"marriage is made up of two great forgivers". The only way this season of conflict and hurt can be walked through is bygrace, granting mercy and forgiveness. Forgiving the hurt and giving mercy, compassion, toward the one who hurt you.

Grace needs to be strapped on during any season of hurt. I have always heard that we forgive not for the offender but for ourselves. Forgiving and giving compassion towards one who has hurt you builds your character and matures you as a person. It also releases you of the burden of hurt.

Determination

The diaper season

I can remember when my kids were in diapers. Potty training was a maniacal chore! I was sure neither of them were ever going to be a normal human and use a toilet! At times, I felt as if they knew they were driving me crazy and refused to use a toilet out of spite! I had to frequently remind myself of this scripture and realize that this season will pass.

Ecclesiastes 3:1 "For everything there is a season,
a time for every purpose under heaven." (KJV)

The adolescent season

This season is fraught with lack of self-confidence, drama, tears, and slamming of doors. Children are stuck between being childhood and adulthood. Leaving behind their childish ways and so desiring to be adults. Our job as parents is to help them navigate this season and spur them on toward all God has for them. At times we have to remind ourselves that all the pain and agony, and at times joy filled moments will someday have a bigger picture as our children grow into adults.

Romans 8:28 "And we know that God causes all things to work together for good to those who love God, to those who are called according to His purpose." (NASB)

Any and all of these seasons take determination. The ability to focus on the season you find yourself in and make the most of the good and bad that come.

In all of these seasons, and others, there is a bigger picture. As you find yourself in a season, asking yourself what is the ultimate goal, it helps you strap on that snowshoe of determination and plow through. Keeping your eye on the prize so to speak.

What season do you find yourself in? Identify it. Speak it out loud. Acknowledge it. Now strap on your snowshoes. Dignity. Grace. Determination.

Rain Boots

It was Girl scout weekend! Every year we went away for a weekend to earn badges for our girl scout sash. We camped, learn to build fires, learn to cook on an open fire, identified different animals and birds in the woods and learned to shape sticks with knives.

This particular weekend, the weather was not cooperating! Rain was forecasted so we all had our girl scout issued rain ponchos. We looked like a herd of baby chickens running around in those ponchos!

It was early evening and we were gathering wood and kindling for our fires. It had been raining but had now stopped. The wind was blowing a bit and it was very ominous outside our tents. None of us really paid much attention at the time. It wasn't until our Girl Scout Leader shouted at us to all get down in the creek bed, then we all panicked! The sky became very dark but outside looked very yellow. I thought maybe it was the reflection of all of us in our bright yellow rain ponchos! Now I know that is what it looks like right before a tornado!

We laid in that creek bed for what seemed like eternity but was in reality only about 10 minutes. A tornado was around us, but not over us! It was quite the adventure for a troop of girl scouts.

Weather related Storms are inevitable. It is a fact of nature. Storms of life are inevitable as well. The true test is not the storm but how we handle the storm.

If you are alive and you are human, you will go through a storm, or two or three. What you want to do is put on those rain boots and make it through the storm! Weather related storms get our shoes wet, our feet wet, we might get cold or snow covered. Regardless, we can still live through it.

In life storms, we're going to get wet and cold, things are going to happen that we're not going to like, but we can persevere through it. We preserve through it realizing God provides for you in the storm; God protects you and there is a bigger picture. There's a process God's taking you through for a reason. You may not always know what that reason is, but He's taking you through it for a reason.

I Hate Storms!

The winter storm

Growing up in the south, in the winter, we had ice storms instead of snow. In the summer due to the heat, we had very loud thunder and lightening storms, and the occasional tornado as depicted in the early part of this chapter!

Growing up, for the Christmas holiday, all we really wanted as kids was a white Christmas! The storm came on quickly but didn't have the white flaky stuff , it had the white clear glassy crystals!

Suddenly I awoke to the sound of a huge thud! It sounded like the world was caving in on my house. A tree had fallen in the ice storm and knocked out our power. Trees were falling everywhere around us. We all piled into our family room on the couch and on the floor, under blankets, with candles for light.

My favorite Christmas gift that year was a Chrissy doll and I hugged her so tightly the every time a tree fell her hair quit growing! (She was on of those dolls that if you pulled her pony tail it would grow, by the way!) I was very glad that I had a doll to hold onto during this winter storm!

The Summer Storm

Every summer, as a teenager, I traveled with my youth group to Jekyll Island, GA for a week of fun in the sun and deepening our faith!

One summer night sitting in our room, all of my roomies and I sat on a bed with the windows wide open watching the lightening cast a blue hue as it touched the ocean.

I wasn't too keen on watching that storm but I do remember thinking and feeling God's presence. We had some much fun

80

just watching the storm, talking about our faith, and what God was doing in our lives. As I reflected on the storms I had endured in the past, I realized that I wasn't enduring this one but rather enjoying it and observing God's hand in it.

Now if I could just see that in the storms of life.

The Recent Storm

2013 was not a good year. I don't know if it is the number 13? I don't usually believe in that stuff. But we had a rough year! IT started out good. Celebrate had a great year end coming into 2013. We were taking the Jay & Laura TV to a new level hoping to reach many more couples. Our calendar was full for the winter. The winter culminated with a sold out show to a venue we had never been before. Jay & I thought this is it. We have crossed the hump, paid our dues, taken it to the next level. We thought " we had arrived".

Within 30 days of that sold out event, we had a conference venue tell us we owed them 30K. We discovered that our booking agent had not been booking us as we thought, and therefore had no gigs for Summer or Fall. We had started 2013 with such promise and excitement and now it was crashing down all around us. We were looking at maybe making a ministry change. It appeared as if doors were opening and we began to pursue them only to have them slam shut.

It is those times when you think you have figured out what the Lord is doing and then you realize you were wrong!

At the same time, we were having personal struggles. Our daughter, 16, on par to be an all state swimmer, developed a back injury that we could not figure out. 6 months of 2013 was filled with different doctors, physical therapy, massage therapists, and holistic doctors. Nothing worked. It was excruciating to watch our daughter walk like an old lady, cry in pain, and miss a 1/3 of her junior swim season.

On the upside of 2013, we gained a daughter in law! NOW that was exciting! Our son Torrey married in the summer of 2013 to the most beautiful God-loving young woman, Shana.

Needless to say, all of these experiences, good and bad, put strain on Jay and I's relationship.

2013 had been a tumultuous roller coaster of emotions!

Pulling into the last days of 2013, I can look back over the year and see God's hand at work.

In early November, Grace experienced healing in her back. She since has been diagnosed with severe Anemia and a dysfunctional gall bladder, all which caused her pain and suffering.

The doors shutting on new ministry direction actually re-focused us back to our hearts' passion to help couples.

We can see how God has used all these little storms to create our utter dependence on Him. As humans we think we can handle most of what Life throws at us. We can figure it all out. For example, with Grace's back we were sure if we just went to this doctor or that doctor or gave her this medicine or essential oil it would work. We spent countless anxious hours trying to figure out what was causing this pain. When we finally realized that the only option was our best option- lay hands on her and pray with the Elders of our church and some close friends, then she experienced healing.

God's protection: Sometimes God's protect is difficult to comprehend, especially in the midst of hurt, rejection, or even loss. We feel like God could have protected us FROM it. As Jay and I thought this past we had an opportunity for a different type of ministry, we took our eyes off of what God had originally called us to do. When the door closed, the circumstances surrounding this opportunity were very hurtful and really caused us a feeling of rejection and betrayal. At the time I wanted to know why God didn't save us from all that? God, why didn't you protect us from this? NOW, looking back I see the closing of this opportunity protected us from a change that was not right for us at all. The door slamming shut clearly gave us the answer, not this trail.

No matter the storm you may find yourself in, God will always protect, always provide for you in the midst of the storm and it His picture, His timing, and we have to trust in Him.

Gods provision: Never once this past year did I question

God's love for me. That isn't to say you might not do the same thru whatever storm you are going thru. However as a result of this entire year, I have begun to pray more and rely more on the promises from scripture . I have realized how much my finite mind can absorb that God does love me inspite of myself. With the marriage of our son, and gaining a daughter in law who loves Jesus and our son, we have been reminded much fathomless God's love is for us.

God's picture: Many times this year Jay and I have wondered and questioned God as to why Grace had to go through this? We still cannot clearly see the bigger picture but some smaller ones have emerged. I can distinctly remember one evening, the three of us sitting on the counters in our kitchen and discussing this illness and the whys and wherefores of it. Grace, in moment of introspection, said "you know maybe it is because swimming has become more important to me that God."

Over the rest of this chapter, I have some friends that are going to share their storms with you. Every one of us goes through a storm in life. Some are just a little rain storm that don't last very long. Others are a tsunami that we take years to recover from and can alter our lives forever.

First I would like to introduce you to Shana. Shana came into my life in 2011 as a contract employee for our ministry while she was a college student. Since then she has become my daughter-in-love, marrying my son Torrey in July of 2013.

My storm started when I was born. My father was abusive to my mom, and so my storm is all about abuse. My father was very abusive to my mom and my mom was terrified of him. This continued for the first five years of my life, and in addition to being physically abusive and mentally abusive, I also had a brother who was abusive to me individually. That was difficult, and it really put our family in a lot of strain.

Looking back and seeing God in that storm, I can say that my mom finally got the strength after being married for five years to my father, to leave his butt behind and move on. And she met my stepdad, who is an amazing man. I call him my dad all the time because he truly stepped up and took that role in my life. He changed everything. He changed our family, taught us how to deal with things we hadn't experienced and how to put the pieces back together. He was constantly encouraging, and gave us hope. He really gave us hope! After experiencing so much abuse and seeing my mom be abused, protecting my sister, and all these things, I learned with Duane, my stepdad how to deal with that, and I also found God has a plan for me moving out beyond and helping other women who are experiencing that.

And Shana does do that, she's been involved in a lot of things where she's helped other women deal with abuse in their lives. So it is a great testimony to how the Lord uses the storms in our lives to make us who we are today.

Next, I would like to introduce you to my friend Tiffany. I first met Tiff at church. Her husband Brad was on staff with Jay and I. I got to know Tiff and cherish her friendship as she and Brad went through their storm.

I've been married to my husband Bradley for 5-years and we have a 1 1/2 year old son, Maximus. And the storm story in my life is actually my husband's' storm. Throughout his life, Bradley struggled with a well hidden, deep rooted issue in his heart that caused him to want to perform for the Lord instead of being in relationship with the Lord. He defined how he could gain acceptance in the world. All of his issues finally surfaced as we became busier with our jobs and birth of our son. This led Bradley to over-work, 60-80 hours a week, and struggling with his severe depression and also experiencing two episodes of near attempted suicide. All this lead to him to being admitted to a mental hospital for suicide watch.

Despite all of this, God made it very clear to me that He was actively seeking my heart during this. He wanted me to go into deeper relationship with Him. And I know that that was for my benefit for sure, but definitely Bradley's as well. Because God wanted me to teach Bradley what it was like to have a true relationship with God without the pressure to perform or without having to work to gain acceptance, because our acceptance is in that undeserving grace of Jesus Christ and His sacrifice; because God loves us with an everlasting love. That will never fade or end. Praise God for that. God just taught me to enjoy being in His presence. Enjoy spending time with Him in the word and prayer.
84

He also told me to take priority in sitting back and listening to God speak to me.

Those ideas at this point in my husband's life were very foreign to him because he was just always in go-mode and rarely sat still. I prayerfully fought for Bradley on a daily basis and tried to create an environment of love and freedom at home so that he could just counteract that bondage that he felt from work. He struggled and eventually hit rock bottom, he finally saw through my faith and strength, that true unconditional love that God taught me, that there is more to life, and that he could see and understand that grace through Jesus Christ. He finally came to understand that you do for the Lord because you are loved, not you are loved because you do. God used that whole situation, and used me to bring about that change in my husband's heart that literally saved his life. Glory to God.

Sometimes our storms that we go through are storms that someone we love is going through. Inevitably it's going to affect us and become our storm. Especially when you're a husband and wife, as Tiff and Brad, that it becomes your storm together.

I would like to introduce to you Mackenzie. Like Tiff, I met Mackenzie while serving with her husband on staff at a local church. She is a bright and vibrant young woman, that I found I had a lot in common.

My storm started much like Shana's, it started when I was born. Mainly with my parent dynamic, my dad who was verbally abusive to our family. I never really understood what a marriage should be like, and because of that and watching my dad, and the relationship I didn't have with him, led me down a path of really just seeking affirmation and love anywhere I could find it.

When I went to college, I literally went off the deep end. I was vice-president of my sorority, thought I had everything together, and was literally into any drug and drinking I could be into. God got ahold of my heart when I hit rock bottom. I know that I had to get to that rock bottom place and be completely broken for me to even hear Him. As a result, it was not only the storm going into that, but the storm in the midst of that and coming out, because all of a sudden when I realized that I was unconditionally loved, everything I had done wasn't going to be held against me.

85

That was a storm in itself, just trying to realize and grasp that it doesn't matter that I have this past that is full of things that I will never want to talk about again, that that's ok because God sees me as what He created me to be and not what I've done. It was really coming to a place here I knew my thoughts and that what I thought of myself was really distorted and learning how to love myself, learning how God loves me and learning how my husband sees me versus how I've seen other men look at me.

Sometimes you're born into a storm, and as a result of that sometimes you make poor choices. Other times the storm you live through is someone else's storm, and sometimes the storm you live through is something you couldn't even imagine, and that's the storm of my friend Wendy.

Wendy, and her husband Steve, is in our small group. We met at a couples' golfing event, and over dinner, she and Steve shared their story.

My storm is and has been the death of my son Owen. He passed away in 2011, at 6 years of age. Just trying to live without someone you don't think you could live without. If someone would've asked me before this happened, I would've said I couldn't live without him. I couldn't. When I had him, he just opened up my heart so much, that I couldn't even imagine not living with him. When he died, we thought we were through our storm. We had our daughter when she was 3-months, Owen was 4, and she was diagnosed with hemangioma in her small intestine. She almost died, but responded incredibly well to treatment. The condition was very rare, doctors had never seen it before in the small intestine. But they decided on treatment, steroids, lots of other stuff and it worked incredibly fast. She responded very well to it. The year preceding Owen's death was really spent working around Emery's health and the fear of "Is she going to be okay?" It became apparent she was responding very well, so we had confidence she was going to be okay. Her year birthday of 2010, they decided that her hemangioma had shrunk, we could take her line out, where she was getting her chemo and that they believed it was done growing. This meant she could be in the water again; Owen and Emery could be in the water together. It had restricted a lot of things we could do with Owen too because of her condition. So I had just gone back to work part-time in January and we thought our life was going to get back to normal.

86

Then all of a sudden in April, Owen got sick with flu-like symptoms we thought, and within a day we took him to a hospital and his body was shutting down and in septic shock. They flew him to DeVos Children's Hospital, but it was too severe and too late, he passed away in April 2011.

From that point on, I would just say that I never thought I could live without Owen. When Emery was sick, I was so grateful that she was doing well, but I didn't turn to God. I didn't turn to God to tell him how thankful I was. I was, but I didn't turn to God even during that experience. I didn't turn to God for comfort. Steve and I were leaning on each other, but it was so different with Owen. When Owen passed away, I just immediately felt different about God. I mean, I think a lot of it was due to the fact that I was shattered, I was so broken. I thought I was in control and everything came out good with Emery. I'd never let anything happen to either one of them. Owen had a peanut allergy, I was so careful with his epi-pen, to make sure it went with him everywhere in his backpack. I was going to make sure that nothing was going to happen to him, and when it did, I think it just shattered that grip of control I thought I had. I realized I didn't have control and I needed something for my broken heart, and Steve couldn't do that for me, Emery couldn't do that for me. It was beyond that and I felt compelled to reach out to God. I felt compelled to read my Bible, which I had never done, and just thinking back on Owen's life and the person he was, it's so obvious to me how God was using him to bring us back to him, to reach us through a little boy that we loved so much.

A storm none of us wants to go through, yet in this fallen world, all of us will experience death. Death of a child is one that is most difficult.

No matter your storm, whether it's a job or a person in your life, death, abuse, whatever your storm, the realizations are the same. God protects you. He's going to provide for you and there's a bigger picture for us to see. Shawna, just tell us how, as you look at the storm and the abuse by your father, but then Duane came into the picture, tell us how you can really look back and see God's protection in that storm.

How do we get through the storms? How do we put on

our rain boots and weather it when it is way bigger than storm we could imagine? In order to handle the storm we have to change our perspective of the storm. We read in Romans 8:28, "For we know that all things work together for the good for those who love God and are called according to HIs purpose." We have to make three realizations. First God works in our storms for our protection. Secondly, He uses those storms to provide for us. Thirdly, the storm is all a part of the bigger picture He has for us. Ultimately the storm will bring us peace.

Our Protection

As we delve deeper into my friends' storms we will see how God used each of their storms for their protection.

Shana: Well, first of all, just the circumstances under which Duane and my mom met, they actually met at a bar. And my mom never went to the bar, and one of her friends convinced her to go out and have a night out and they met and that night Duane told his friend he was going to marry her. That in itself is a miracle, a miracle meeting. And just that Duane had experienced so many of the things that me and my sister had experienced, living with my biological dad, going through all of that abuse, God's hand on him. Duane is a Christian, hates going to church, he's a man of contradiction, but when it came to me and my sister, he loved us unconditionally, which is the way I learned how God loves me, is because I saw that through Duane. So God's hand was on it the entire time, God's hand is on me and my family and even like I said, looking forward, I want to work to advocate for women who are going through those issues and that's God, because I couldn't do that on my own.

Again we see through interesting circumstances how God protects. Some of us would say, God would never go to a bar, but we forget Jesus turned water into wine at a wedding, so let's just remember that. God used a miracle meeting like Shana said, to bring someone into her life to bring protection. That is God, bringing protection through Duane. Remember, it doesn't matter the circumstance, God's still going to protect.

Tiff: God just protected my heart during all of this. Bradley needed a rock to be there and bounce ideas off, be there as his main support, besides God obviously. But God gave me such
88

amazing peace that surpasses all understanding, so that during this whole time I was not scared or worried. I knew deep in my heart that God was going to protect us and take care of us. He showed me on a daily basis how much he loves me, and showed me in the word different verses to help me get through. My all-time favorite verse is 2 Corinthians 4:16-17, "Therefore we do not lose heart. Though outwardly we are wasting away, inwardly we are being renewed day by day. For our light in momentary troubles are achieving for us an eternal glory that far outweighs them all. So we fix our eyes not on what is seen but what is unseen, because what is seen is temporary but what is unseen is eternal." So that's what God got me through.

We can see God's protection through the fact that Bradley is still being with us, through two suicidal moments. He is still with us and God did protect Bradley through a wife that loved him through it. Even if you're in it together, the Lord will use that protection. He's going to protect you through it.

Mackenzie: It's funny. I feel like there are so many areas that I saw God's protection. One of the ironic ones that I feel like people are bashful about, is He protected my body. He protected me especially with the amount of guys that I slept with. He protected me. That blows me away every time I think of it. I know what should've happened. I know the consequences, and I know the situations I put myself in when I didn't know Him. I would go out and make decisions that if my daughter or friends made, I mean I wouldn't be happy with them! I made really bad decisions yet He protected me. Even though I didn't love Him and know Him, He was there.

God had a plan for Mackenzie's life. He loved her before she love him and he protected her to accomplish his purpose in her life.

Wendy: It's an interesting thing when someone you love dies, because I think of protection as physical protection, and when death happens, it's shocking and it's kind of like, where was the protection for Owen? But I instantly felt like Owen was protected. I felt like I couldn't live with myself without him. I second guessed myself and what-if'd the situations over and over, but I had a feeling in my heart that God was protecting Owen. I didn't understand it and I think as I turn to the Bible, I think that God protects and is more concerned with our eternal/soul, you know, and I think our bodies are going to die. The disciples almost all died young, and Jesus told them,"Don't fear those that kill the body. They can't touch the soul." When I read that, I felt that is what God is protecting.

The change in my heart towards God, since Owen's passing, I can't deny it. I couldn't say that I loved God before. I believed in God and Jesus, but I can't say that I loved him. When Owen was born, he brought something into our lives that I didn't know we were missing. Even from the time he was a little baby, he was so smart and just quiet, but he was always thinking. We sent him to St. Mary's preschool, so he went to a catholic preschool and became very interested in religion and he talked about God a lot. He talked about when he goes to the clouds and what's going to be there. And I would say "Owen, you won't be in the clouds until you're an old man. You don't need to worry." I look back at that and I see that as God preparing Owen, and preparing me even though I would not think or didn't want to go there.

I have a picture of Owen with his favorite toy, a red transformer. He loved Transformers, he was the Transformers master. He became interested in those when he was 2. But it's so perfect to me, but he was the ultimate little transformer in our lives.

Owen wanted a Bible the Christmas before he passed away, and we didn't have a Bible in the house. I think Steve had one from catechism, but we weren't church goers. But he wanted a Bible, so we bought him a Bible. He would draw pictures of Jesus being the best gift ever. I wasn't leading him that way, but I think God was.

A week before Owen died, he walked into the kitchen and said"Mommy, you know Jesus died on the cross for us?" I was cleaning up and I said yeah I do, buddy. And off he went to play and little did I know, how important that would become. It means everything.

God Provides

God protects us through our storms. God also provides for us during those storms. He provides what we need at the moment that we need it.

Shana: Gosh, I have seen God's provision non-stop. From the very practical things, such as how does a single mom with two kids afford to buy a house? Then Duane came into our lives. Before he even met us, because mom wouldn't let him meet us, my mom told him that she didn't have money for winter jackets for us and my dad wouldn't give her the money. Duane went out and bought jackets. Not only jackets, but Mickey Mouse jackets and we loved Mickey Mouse!

Providing the practical things such as winter jackets, but He also provided for my heart needs. I partied and got drunk, and I see God's protection so much in that. I was never caught drinking underage, all these things that could've happened, even just God protecting my heart. My biological dad still sneaks into the picture every now and then. God is protecting my heart and physical protection.

God provides through our storms not only in physical ways, yet emotional as well. Giving us what we need for our body, yet also providing for our heart needs.

Tiff: God provided in a couple of different ways. For me personally, one way would be he surrounded me with Godly women in my life that could help support me through prayer and encouragement and to know I have somebody who's got my back. Another way is financially. For probably the majority of this 2-year period that we were struggling and Bradley was having a hard time, we were living paycheck-to-paycheck and mainly dependent upon my income.

We had a perfect storm weekend I call it, where I was to get paid on Friday. We had a couple bills scheduled to be paid online that Friday, and on the following Monday we had the two biggest bills to be paid, and for whatever reason, my paycheck didn't come through. And we did not have enough money to get us through the Monday and it was the weekend so we couldn't do anything about it, couldn't go to the bank at all. What did God do? Well we just prayed and prayed, and I just knew in my heart that God would provide for us and I really didn't know how. So by the time Monday rolled around, God provided enough money to pay for everything and we actually had $11 leftover. And that's abundant living in my opinion.

At times when we are in a storm, the end is not in sight, but we watch God provide in miraculous ways. Storms are not fun, but it is fun to watch God work like he did for Brad and Tiff.

Mackenzie: I think the main way that God has provided for me was bringing a husband who is incredible. Even after I accepted Christ and started to learn how God saw me as His daughter. I didn't believe I would be provided with a man that would see me that way, or at least see me how I was now. I thought would be given a man that obviously wanted to know about my past, and wanted to compare himself to what happened and the reality is that Mitch is the closest thing that I'll ever experience to Jesus on this earth. It's been amazing, I feel like that time after time. Even our dating experience, how we met and married, everything was so orchestrated. It's undeniable, when I tell the story. When I go back and read my journals and see, I didn't even ask questions, it just all fell into place and it really was a fairy tale. We know that marriage isn't always a fairy tale, but at least I feel like the majority of my love story really has been provided by God and I couldn't have even imagined that.

Even when our storm is the result of bad choices on our part, God still provides for us in ways more beautiful than we can imagine or think we deserve.

Wendy: I had long-time friends that were so committed to being there for me. They would just come and set with me, let me cry and run through the crazy things that run through your head. They would listen to me. And if I said" I can't stop reading", they would come with books. They would do anything they could do to help. These were friends I had most of my life and those friendships changed so much after Owen died too. I don't remember discussing God much at all with my friends prior to that. We were all believers, but it wasn't something we shared, and that has changed so much. They have been such supporters and encouragers that way too.

I look at the people that God was bringing into our lives even before Owen passed away. Gene and Wendy Smith, you and Jay; I know that's not coincidence that that happened. My sister knew Wendy, she was using her as a daycare provider; Storm had bought her son's business. I can see God was bringing them into our lives because you guys have been so essential to helping heal through this, to know that we have friends we can pray with and that are praying for us, and that love God. And if you would've told me that me and Steve would be setting in a small group with you guys five years before, I would have said no way. That's not cool, we could not be doing that. And Steve would've said the same thing. So I can see these changes that there's no way we would've done that before.

God also provided for us financially in a crazy way. We were at the end of our rope financially. I had to stop working when Emery was sick. I stayed home for a year.

We had issues with the house we bought, so we were at the end of our line there. All of a sudden I win a sweepstakes. I kept thinking, this is so weird, this isn't real, and it was. When we came home from the hospital, the check was in the mailbox. And that was hard for me at first, because I felt like it was associated with that, and I felt like I want to rip it up, but we needed it.

God provided over and over. The sweepstakes allowed me to stay home and continue to take care of Emery. It allowed me to stay home to make the friendships and these relationships that I needed, because I wouldn't have otherwise. I would have gone back to work, I wouldn't have read my Bible and become so prayerful about things. It allowed me to be kind of still and focus on that and I needed that because I'm not someone who would reach out to someone as a friend.

In our storms, God protects us. He provides for us. He always has our best interest in mind, even though we can't always see it.

God's Picture

I think the hardest thing sometimes when we go through a storm is realizing that God does have a bigger picture. We don't always want to see that, because we don't really like the storm we're in and we don't understand, why does a 6-yr old boy die? And why do I have to make the choices I make? Why does my husband have to suffer through what he's suffering through? Why did my mom and my sister and I have to suffer? We ask all these questions, but there's a bigger picture. The storm is a process of one small part of a much bigger picture. Sometimes we don't see that picture or even part of it until we get through the storm. Some-times we get glimpses in the midst of the storm. Yet we must rely on God and trust in His bigger picture for our lives.

   Shana: The bigger picture from my storm is now I work with the church in a Redemption ministry, which is focused on helping specifically, women deal with some of these issues like abuse, bad decisions, and issues like these. Just to see God's light in the midst of that and help them heal and move forward.

   In addition to that, I work with a group called SAPA, who are peer advocates on Central Michigan University's campus, helping people who have experienced sexual abuse. I am using the experience that I had and understanding that experience and seeing God in it. Relying on God for all the strength to help the women that I'm helping now and looking to the future, I want to continue doing this. This is what I know God has created me to do and all these experiences has put me to the point where I want to help other people who are experiencing it. So that is God's bigger picture in my life.

   Tiff: The bigger picture for me I could wrap-up very easily with 1 Corinthians 10:31, "Whether, then, you eat or drink or whatever you do, do all to the glory of God. (NASB) You can face lots of different circumstances, but in everything just look to God. Change your perspective, because it's important to look at what God IS doing, not what he's NOT doing.

   For me, personally, I've learned to look at it that way because I feel like I'm a joy carrier. I try to find joy in everything. There's so many circumstances and situations that we don't know about or just can't see, whether around us or in the spiritual world, we just know that God is working for our good in everything that we do. So I would encourage people to just be somebody who is a glass overflowing person and not a glass half empty person.

   Mackenzie: For me, the bigger picture defines my life. Everything that I've been through, I have already seen God use to affect someone else, or to let me able to tell a story, or identify with a woman who comes to me in tears and she's like, "I'm never going to be forgiven for this", or "this man will never enter my life because look at who I am", or "look at what I've done". And for me to be able to actually use an example and say, "No, you're not. There's truth you don't know yet." Everything that Mitch and I do as a couple, we're able to testify to what God has done in our lives

94

and our walk. And I know for me, I don't think I was truly healed, and there's still stuff that comes up, let's be honest, but I don't think I was truly at a point where I felt healed until I started working with others and listening to girls and asking the questions and saying it's ok to tell me about this because people aren't perfect, Christians aren't perfect, and just to be real and authentic. And say, I made mistakes, I'm not this pastor's wife that you think I am. So just using it every single day, and I wouldn't trade any of it for the world at this point.

Wendy: I see it in Steve and I and who we are, and where our hearts are. Before I would say we were pretty selfish and we were close minded on our kids and that, and I think all of that changed and I think I see God's presence so much more in my friends, that I wasn't really looking for before.

Owen's life, it was brief, he was only here for 6-years, but I feel like in his 6-yrs, he has touched so many people. Just the things he came with, things I wasn't putting there, that God put in him to share, that we can now share. He transformed our lives, our hearts, and when he died, it allowed Jesus to transform our hearts, that we didn't realize we needed that, we didn't realize we were missing that.

Four very lovely women all with different storms that have affected their lives in ways unimaginable. Whatever the storm you are going through, remember that God's going to protect you and he's going to provide for you in ways you may not have even thought about yet, and there's a bigger picture to the storm. There's a reason for the storm.

Romans 8:28, "And we know that God causes all things to work together for good to those who love God, to those who are called according to *His* purpose." (NASB) The death of a child, the suicidal attempt of a husband and depression, bad choices, abuse by a father, all those things work together for the good to those that love God and are called according to his purpose.

The next storm you go through: God will protect you. He will provide for you. Remember there is a bigger picture involved. But the end result is peace. Peace that guards your heart and passes all understanding in our human minds.

We live in Michigan, in the winter we endure frequent snow

storms. Some storms are gentle and quiet and others harsh and violent. When it's all said and done, the next day my favorite thing to do is strap on my snowshoes, go out and take some time to enjoy the peaceful quiet that is after the storm. That's what I would encourage you to do, is as you go through the storm, realize God's going to protect you, going to provide for you, there's always a bigger picture and there's always peace after every storm.

Hiking Boots

I remember as a young girl playing with a magic 8 ball. It was a black ball with an 8 on one side and and box on the other. You would ask the "8" a question, turn the ball over and it would give you an answer. It was great fun and sometimes I even wondered if that answer would come true.

What would you do different, how would you live if you could see into a magic ball and could see what your life held?

I am not sure I would want to see my entire life mapped out before me! As I reflect on the twists and turns I have navigated on this journey called life, the adventure has been in the unknown.

One step at a time is best how we live this journey. We do not know exactly where the trail goes but we do know that the One who made the trail is faithful. We don't know where the trail may lead but we do know who made the trail and He is guiding our steps. My life verse is very appropriate here:
Jeremiah 29:11 For I know the plans I have for you declares the Lord, plans to prosper you and not to harm you. Plans to give you a hope and a future.

As we hike the journey that God has laid out for us we need to remember to stay on our trail- the one He has planned for us. We also need to realize that we have our own equipment that is different from others. God has uniquely equipped you to hike the journey He has for you. Lastly remember that He has you on this journey to prosper you and to give you hope. Keep your eye on Him, He is the trail guide that will be with you every step you take.

The Best Hike of My Life

July 4, 1984 I met the man of my dreams! Jay and I were set up on a blind date by one of my best friends, Deaver Corzine and her husband, Chaz.

Jay showed up at my house with long dark curly hair wearing purple plaid shorts and a purple polo shirt. I answered the door with dripping wet hair and shorts and a t-shirt. He was early and I was definitly not ready for our date!

We went to an Atlanta Braves baseball game, talked the entire game. At the end of the game, the obligatory July 4th fireworks went off. I wondered if it was a sign?! After the fireworks were done, the entire stadium was dark so I grabbed Jay's hand as we made our way out of the stadium There was an instant connection but I was not sure where this would actually go.

The next morning at breakfast I told my mom I was going to marry Jay! She choked on her Cheerios! I just felt in my heart that he was the one.

Ten days later he asked me to marry him! BUT....that is jumping ahead!

After our blind date, I invited him to a putt putt outing with my college group at church. He passed on the invite. However, the next day he asked me out to see the movie, Ghostbusters. I accepted his invitation. Come to find out he just needed to get out of Chaz and Deaver's house for the evening as they were having guests over for dinner!

For the next 10 days, I managed to make our paths cross at various events: Bible studies, social gatherings, etc. He jokes and tells people I stalked him....and perhaps I did a little!

However, on July 14th, he asked me to marry him! There was no ring or engagement photos, just a simple question with an enthusiastic answer.

After our summer jobs were over, we made plans to attend a youth camp in Woodland Park, CO that Jay's dad ran. I had never been to Colorado, so I was thoroughly excited to spend a week in the Rocky Mountains.

As our trip drew closer, our best friends at the time, Dean Moyer and Andrea Grayson Corley, would randomly say to me, " Remember it all happened at the foot of the cross." I would smile at them and reply, " I know" while in my mind I was trying to figure out what was wrong with them! I knew Jesus and I knew what He did for me on the cross, why were Dean and Andrea reminding me all the time?
98

Our trip to Colorado from Atlanta was a long hot 24 hour car ride in Jay's little Toyota Tercel. We drove straight through the night and arrived in Woodland Park around lunch time.

Our entire ride out, Jay and been talking about Soldiers Mountain, the centerpiece of Quaker Ridge Camp. The plan was for us to get a picnic lunch, drive up to Quaker Ridge, and make the hike up Soldiers to see the view, before others arrived in camp.

We stopped at a Pizza Hut in town for a picnic pizza that we put in my backpack. As we pulled into Quaker Ridge, Jay pointed upwards to this beautiful mountain, and exclaimed "That is where we are going!" I was excited make the hike.

Understand this is not a walk in the park, this is a steep hike up the side of a mountain in Colorado! It took us about an hour to make the climb. As we reached the top, I was so enamored with the view that I neglected to see the cross at the top of the mountain. Eventually, I took my eyes off the view and turned around to see the cross, and laying at the foot of it, was a single red rose. " Why is there a rose up here", I asked. Jay encouragde me to go over to the cross and find out. The rose was lying on it's side with a card attached to it. I picked it and read it, "Congratulations! Love Dean & Andrea" I was still trying to process what this was for, when I looked up and Jay was on one knee with a ring in his hand, proposing once again!

Now, we had just driven 24 long hot hours across the country in a little car, going from sea level to over 9000 feet. We had hiked an hour up a mountain, and we had eaten cold doughy pizza.

When Jay asked the question, I was feeling the altitude and was a bit confused by all that was happening, so I did not answer right away. Before I could form the word "yes" to his question, altitude sickness took over and instead of answering him, I puked on him, and the ring!

Dean and Andrea were right! It all happened at the foot of the cross!

We are all on a journey, sometimes it is a straight path without too many twists and turns, and other times we can't see where we are going but we journey on one step at a time.

The Do's and Don'ts of Hiking

Stay on the trail

Your life, your journey, is your trail designed specifically for you, created by God who created you uniquely you!

We all have a different trail to hike in this life. We have been created equal yet different. We have different gifts and abilities, talents, and personalities. These all contribute to the trail that God has designed for us. When we try to be something we are not, we get off our trail and onto someone else's. A trail we are not equipped to hike.

"Do not be afraid to be different from other people. The path I have called you to travel is exquisitely right for you. The more closely you follow My leading, the more fully I can develop your gifts"
Young, Sarah (2004-10-12). Jesus Calling (p. 212). Thomas Nelson. Kindle Edition.

We all have an innate human tendency, a desire to be different. Not different from the world but rather different from who we have been created to be. We tend to see others gifts and abilities clearer than we see our own. We see the life someone else lives and wish we could live it. Instead we need to focus on what God has given us in our life and what He has equipped us to do. When we can take time to see in our own life how God has moved and worked then we begin to see the path He has us on.

My first God-sighting

I was the first in my family to attend college. My sister, Sandy, had spent some time studying at a local community college, but I was the first to leave home in hopes of attaining a four year degree. Money was tight in our family. My dad was disabled

100

and my mom worked both inside the home and outside the home. She was a kindergarten teacher and then an executive secretary/assistant in an insurance firm. She also did alterations and sewing for people as a side job to make ends meet.

I did not apply but to two colleges my senior year of high school. I applied to Montreat Anderson College and to the University of Georgia. In high school, I was a good student. I always got A's and B's. When I received my rejection letter from the University of Georgia, I was devasted! I could not understand how with my grades and my SAT score I was rejected. It did not make sense. So I moved on.

I attended Montreat Anderson College. At that time, MAC was just a 2 year college. MAC is located in the spectacular Blueridge mountains, east of Asheville, NC. Montreat was and is a magical place! If it sounds familar to you that would be because it is the home of Billy Graham.

As a young woman away from home for the first time it was a perfect setting. Lake Susan surrounded by a beautiful old stone building. All the buildings on campus were built of fieldstone. MAC was and is a Christian college. This was a place where I thrived. I really came into my own there. I discovered more about the Lord and about myself. As is a frequent sentiment among Montreatians, I never wanted to leave!

The first time I remember God answering a prayer for me in a tangible way was my sophomore year in college. Right before Christmas break of my sophomore year, I was informed that I was not going to be able to afford to return to MC. I was devastated! I knew my mother could not afford to pay for college. I had all the grants I could get. Yet I also knew this is where the Lord wanted me! I now had come to understand that the rejection from UGA was God directing me where He wanted me to go. Had I got accepted at UGA I would have gone there. That was the plan afterall. But when I was not accepted I decided MAC was a good second choice. Now a year and a half into school, I knew it was the best choice and the one God wanted for me. I knew all I could do was pray. If God wanted me at Montreat, then He would have to provide the money.

I still to this day do not know where the money came from,

but over Christmas break, I was informed by Montreat that the monies had come in and I could come back for my last semester at Montreat!

Montreal was a huge part of my journey and I knew that God wanted me there! This was part of my journey to hike.

Be still and know...

Many times in life we can't see what God has for us, and He has uniquely created us because we are moving at lightening speed on our journey!

Psalm 46:10 Be Still and know that I am God

I grew up at North Avenue Presbyterian Church in Atlanta, GA. I am eternally thankful for the rich spiritual heritage I was surrounded with and the traditions and values that were instilled in from birth until young adulthood.

Dr. Vernon Broyles was the senior pastor and Rev. Cook Freeman was the Associate Pastor. Both men of God, very loving and filled with grace. I will never forget the impact of these two men on my life. NAPC is a very large downtown church. 5 stories full of history and wonderful people! I remember as a young person being awed by the majesty of the building and feeling so safe because of the people in the church. Also as a young person it was a great place to run around in! It has many nooks and crannies to explore.

One of my fondest memories of these two gentleman was the scripture they always quoted whenever they would see me in the hallway at church. It didnt matter which one it was, they would stop me, place a hand on my head or shoulder and say " I will give you a quarter if you can stand still for one minute" and then they would quote Psalm 46:10 " Be still and know that I am God". I can't remember ever getting a quarter but I do remember that verse.

I remembered that verse when I did not get into the college of my choice. I remembered that verse when my dad feel and broke his good leg. I remembered that verse when a relationship ended. I remembered that verse when my dad died. I remembered that verse when I met Jay.

That verse has carried me thru many trials in my life and many joyous times as well. It has come to mind whenever I am anxious, and whenever I need to let go. It is forever etched on my heart and mind all because these two men took the time to quote it to my young heart.

This verse also encapsulates who I am and who God created me to be.

Use your equipment

Snow Flakes

As I am writing this book, there is a gentle snow falling outside. I am watching in awe with the realization that each snowflake I see, which are too numerous to even count, are uniquely different from the next. Our creator made it so. As He did us.

We are each uniquely different. Some differences are more subtle others much more noticeable. It is easy to see gender differences, and skin color differences. Even fraternal twins have been created with subtle differences that sometimes the human eye cannot detect right away but the differences are still there. I have a friend that has twin daughters, Abigail and Madeline. Abby is the oldest of the two and thus the leader. Maddy being the youngest is the follower. According to Angie, the girls' mom, Abby displays many qualities of a little mother, while Maddy is more like the child. Maddy is a lover. She will snuggle with anyone who is willing to wrap their arms around her. Abby likes to learn and Maddy likes to play.

Just like a snowflake, we have been created unique. God has designed us with our gifts and abilities to use on our journey. As is stated in Jeremiah, He has a plan for each and everyone of us. Uniquely equipping us for a purpose.

Lest we forget, Jesus had a journey to hike as well. One

that He was created to live and uniquely equipped by God the Father to give His life for us. He is the trail guide, walking with us every step we take.

Jesus' Journey

Jesus' less than triumphant birth - the Jewish people were looking for a savior a King, in their frame of reference, the way they understood a king to be. They were looking for a man to rise up to great power, to be clothed in the finest of cloth. Wear a crown and a robe of extravagance. What they got was a baby born of a virgin, a questionable pregnancy. This young mother was not married. She gave birth to Jesus in a stable. A stinky smelly stable. No doctors, or nurses, or midwife. Just these unmarried teenagers.

Not the journey the Jewish people thought their king would hike, but the one God knew He would.

Keep your eye on the trail guide

2013, the year that was and thank God never will be again!

Part of the journey, is strapping on those hiking boots thru the good and the bad parts of the trail. 2013 was one of those years for me. It was year of good parts of the trail and some not so good parts.

2013 kicked off with our son, Torrey, informing us of his engagement! Now that is a good part of the trail! Shana had been working for our ministry in a very part time position for almost 8 months before Torrey even met her. When we interviewed her for the part time job in Nov. of 2011, I commented to Jay that she was the perfect match for Torrey! And as some mothers can do I went about trying to make the "meet" happen! My attempts were not very successful so I decided it was time to let the Lord do it.

Needless to say they met the following summer, dated a short time in the fall of 2012, and announced to us in the winter of 2013 that they were going to be married that summer! See mom always knows best!

The joy of a wedding, and acquiring a daughter-in-law was a great part of the journey in 2013.

A Not So Great Part

2013 found Jay and I in two different worlds. We were continuing in our own ministry, Celebrate Ministries, speaking and traveling around the country presenting our Ultimate Date Nights. However, for the better part of a year, we also had our feet in a local church ministry.

We thoroughly enjoyed being a part of a team of people doing ministry together. We were consulting with this local church in Marriage and Family Ministry, including men's and women's ministry as well. We loved investing in the lives of the young staff and their families. It was a whole new world for us and to be honest we were surprised that we enjoyed it so much.

As the ministry continued at the church, our speaking ministry with Celebrate was struggling. Circumstances unbeknownst to us at the time and beyond our control were shortchanging our schedule and we were finding ourselves more and more at the church.

Thus the question arose in our hearts and minds, " Was the Lord steering us into a new chapter of our lives?" It looked good in the reality of life. Our daughter was in her Junior year of high school and very active. With Jay and I home more it gave a bit of a semeblance of normalcy to her life. Not that she ever minded our travel.

We were really enjoying what we were doing at the church. We were building teams to do ministry together. We were implementing programs for married couples, men and women. Working in a church was something we never thought we were cut out to do but we actually loved it!

Circumstances began to look like the Lord was taking us in a new direction to be full time at the church. We began to dream and plan accordingly. Then in an instant all that changed. The rug was yanked out from under us and now we had to pick up the pieces and move on.

When something like this happens, there are feelings of hurt and anger to deal with. There is the questioning in your soul, were we not listening Lord?

The reality is on this journey of life we know who holds the future. We may think we know what the future holds, but we never really do. In hindsight, the events of 2013 were a blessing in disguise. We are more focused, rejuvenated, and excited for the future of our ministry, Celebrate Ministries.

Did the Lord orchestrate 2013 just for that reason? We may never be able to fully answer that question in human terms but we did strap on our hiking boots and follow the path He laid out before us.

Jeremiah 29:11 For I know the plans I have for you declares the Lord, plans to prosper you and not to harm you. Plans to give you a hope and a future.

Barefoot

Jay and I often talk to couples about the fact that one of them will stand over the grave of the other. Not in an attempt to be morbid but to be real. We will all stand over the grave of our spouse. Unless you die at the same time, and if that happens to us, it will be because I am driving!

Jay says if he goes first he doesn't want to be lying down in the casket but rather sitting up, smiling and holding a sign that says " I Did". I ran the race, I fought the good fight.

We all come into the world barefoot and we all go out of the world barefoot- what matters is how we live in between. Will you be able to say I ran the race God put before me? Will you be able to say I had to courage to fight the good fight?

When I leave this world barefoot, I don't want to leave my kids an enormous amount of money or a house on the beach. I want to leave them a legacy of laughing in the midst of trials, loving Jesus first, then others, and living life in such a way that they leave an impactful legacy as well.

We may leave this world barefoot but we need to also live in this world barefoot. We do this by taking three actions: Laugh often, love always, and leave a legacy.

Laughing often

In Proverbs we read that laughter is like good medicine. When we laugh, we are releasing endorphins into our bodies, a natural opiate. In other words, when we laugh we are drugging ourselves!

Sometimes in life we take ourselves way too seriously. Understandably, there are situations in life that are not comical nor funny, but laughing can get us through those times.

Laughter is good for our hearts and our souls.

Loving always

Being present in the moment. Social media and smartphones have made this a different world than it used to be. I saw a post just the other day on Facebook by a teacher. She had given her students a writing assignment and she was getting texts from her student with questions about the assignment. When she started teaching she didn't even have a phone in her classroom!

Times are changing and we have to change with them.

It is easy when you are with people, to have your smart phone in your hand checking your texts or social media outlets instead of being actively involved in the conversation.

Just the other day we were on a phone call with our daughter who is away at college. We had her on speakerphone, Jay had his computer out checking his email! Now he didn't miss anything she said but it is about being present in the moment.

Loving always is also about being transparent with those around you. Authenticity in this life is hard to come by. On our Facebook pages we can live vicariously through others. We can post statuses and pictures that make us look cooler and hipper than our "friends".

Transparency is about allowing others to see your hurts, your joys and who you are at your core.

I am not a hugger or a crier. I prided myself on living in a bubble and protecting my heart from others. I only allowed people to see whom I wanted them to see. I have learned over the years that this is not an authentic, transparent life.

I always wanted people to see me as the fun loving happy go lucky southern girl who had life under control. But the reality was totally the opposite. I loved having fun, but my life wasn't fun. Growing up, my family struggled because of my dad's many illnesses. I wanted life to be happy and easy so I projected that outwardly. I wanted people to think I had a "normal" dad.

It has only been in the last several years that I realized

there is more to me than I allow others to see. Experiencing my pains have made me stronger. My family growing up made me who I am today, so I have the ability to genuinely encourage others. When I cry it allows others to see inside my heart.

Being present in the moment and allowing others to see who you are brings an authenticity to this world that it craves.

Leaving a legacy

One of my favorite songs ever is by the artist Steve Green, *" may the footprints that we leave lead them to believe and the lives we live inspire them to obey".*

I remember the first time I heard the song, the picture that came to mind was footprints on the beach. I saw a picture I had seen many times before. A picture that had two sets of footprints on the beach because Jesus was walking alongside of me. Another picture I saw had only one set of footprints when Jesus was carrying me.

Are we living in our lives in such a way that those around us see those times that we are walking with Jesus and also seeing those times when He has to carry us? Are we leaving footprints that allow those who come after us to know that we had a faith that allowed us to journey onto the most extraordinary life?

My friend Karen has already left this world barefoot. She died from cancer several years ago. The legacy she left lives on in the life of her husband, children and now grandchildren.

She was a strong woman who lived an extraordinary life. She knew what God has gifted her to do and she did it with abandon. She loved her family and her friends in such a away that her legacy inspires others.

At her funeral, we were all given a paper with a butterfly inside. After the service, we all gathered by the river, opened our papers and let the butterfly go! It was a beautiful sight to behold.

I was reminded that caterpillars are not always the most

lovely creatures. They can be furry and slimy. They get stepped on. Yet they have a job to do. Wrap themselves up in a cocoon, to become one of the most delicate yet beautiful creatures God created.

We may start this extraordinary journey as a caterpillar. Life happens, we cocoon around ourselves. Choose to live the life created for you and you will emerge as the beautiful woman God created you to be.

Take your first steps today to your extraordinary life!